WHY I BELIEVE

Roger Carswell

Copyright © 2018 by Roger Carswell

First published in Great Britain in 2018

British Library Cataloguing in Publication Data
A record for this book is available from the British Library

ISBN: 978-1-911272-97-7

Cover design by Mike Thorpe
Typeset by Jude May

Printed 2019 in Denmark by Nørhaven

10Publishing, a division of 10ofthose.com
Unit C, Tomlinson Road, Leyland, PR25 2DY, England
Email: info@10ofthose.com
Website: www.10ofthose.com

Dedication

To the memory of my parents, William and Rhoda Carswell

And

*To all who refuse to be manipulated by the media and so don't
buy into the prevailing tide which turns a deaf ear to the voice
of God, a blind eye to the love of Jesus and a hard heart to the
invitation of the Holy Spirit who says, 'Come and see.'*

Contents

Acknowledgements

I want to take this opportunity to express my appreciation to Mrs Christine Watts of Leeds. She has carefully typed and improved the original manuscript, showing great patience throughout. Her life and work is a demonstration of the vigour God gives to those who believe. I am grateful too to my wife, Dot, to the late Jean Smith, Ossie Ross and Mark Wallace who have each improved on the text with their comments, corrections and insights, and my now deceased parents, who patiently improved the original edition of this book. In innumerable ways they were my mentors.

Introduction

The Bible does not seek to prove God's existence; it treats it as fact. The Bible's opening words are: 'In the beginning God ... '[1]

It has to be the most frequently discussed issue. From schoolchildren to senior citizens, the argument as to whether or not God exists fuels the flames for heated debate. The Bible does not give space to weighing the arguments. It claims to be the Word of God and so renders unnecessary the discussion. In fact, the Bible teaches that there is a basic dishonesty in the heart of every atheist. 'Only fools say in their hearts, "There is no God"' or, as the thrust of the meaning of the verse implies, the fool has said in his heart, 'No God for me.'[2] In other words, it is not so much that people *cannot* believe, but that they *will* not. In the New Testament part of the Bible, we read:

[T]hey can clearly see his invisible qualities – his eternal power and divine nature. So they have no excuse for not knowing God. Yes, they knew God, but they wouldn't worship him as God or even give him thanks. And they began to think up foolish ideas of what God was like. As a result, their minds became dark and confused. Claiming to be wise, they instead became utter fools. And instead of worshipping the glorious, ever-living God, they worshipped idols made to look like mere people and birds and animals and reptiles. So God abandoned them to do whatever shameful things their hearts desired.[3]

God has revealed Himself to the people He has made.

Of course, we will never, as finite beings, be able to understand fully all the qualities and attributes of the infinite God. God is too great for little humans like us to reach, and He is too holy for us to approach. However, God has revealed Himself and reached down to rescue us.

God has revealed Himself to us in many ways, but here are five which are basic:

- Through creation – the material word;
- Through conscience – the unspoken word;
- Through Scripture – the written word;
- Through Christ – the living and loving Word; and
- Through Christian conversion – the experienced word.

In this book we will explore some of these aspects of God's revelation to His world. We will merely scrape the surface of evidence, which in totality is vast. The apostle John wrote at the end of his gospel, 'Jesus also did many other things. If they were all written down, I suppose the whole world could not contain the books that would be written.'[4] However, the Bible speaks of 'many infallible proofs' concerning Christ and His rising from the dead.[5] The evidence of the truth of the gospel is overwhelming, and may be experienced by those who sincerely seek God.

On 25 August 1965, I became a Christian. I shall never forget that day. As a teenager I was on holiday in the Lebanon, staying with relatives who were involved in Christian medical work in Beirut and beyond. Their consistent character and caring lives made a deep impression upon me. I began to ask myself questions such as, 'What is a Christian?', 'Why are these people so different from me?' and 'Why do they live for others and I for myself?'

I had been brought up in a home where my parents had taught

me about God and Jesus and had set a fine example of Christian behaviour. However, as a young person I had drifted away from living life as God would expect. My life and language spoke of a deep-down restlessness and rebellion. But I knew that there was more to life than living for the moment.

After a game of tennis, an uncle of mine began to chat through the gospel message. Using a pocket New Testament he explained step by step my position before God, and God's method of bringing me into a relationship with Himself. He showed me in the Bible Romans 3:23 and asked me to read aloud the words: 'for all have sinned and fall short of the glory of God'. I was well aware of wrong within. My attitude to God, my parents and others was far from what I knew to be right. God's holiness and my sinfulness were a reality to me.

We turned to Romans 6:23, and again I read aloud: 'For the wages of sin is death, but the gift of God is eternal life in Christ Jesus our Lord.' My uncle explained how sin not only separated me from God now, but ultimately would condemn me to hell. Then he explained to me the significance of Jesus' death on the cross. God's great rescue mission was bound up in Jesus Christ coming to earth. God Himself had stooped to enter our world in the person of Christ. Again, we looked in Romans. This time it was chapter 5 verse 8: 'But God demonstrates his own love toward us, in that while we were still sinners, Christ died for us.'

Graphically, he explained that God had placed my sin on Jesus. He was the substitute dying in my place, paying for my sin. I had never understood that before. I felt that if God loved me enough for Christ to die for me, then the least I should do was trust Him.

Jesus Christ not only died, but rose again. Things began to fall into place in my mind. Jesus had died to offer me forgiveness, and three days later had risen. He was therefore able not only to

13

forgive me, but give me His power over sin and death. God, by His Holy Spirit, could come and live in my life.

Simply, sitting on a log in the mountains of Lebanon, overlooking Beirut, I prayed, placing my trust in Jesus. I thanked Him for dying for me, and asked Him to forgive me and make me His forever. There was no flash in the sky – but neither was this a flash in the pan!

God became real to me and totally changed my aims, ambitions and affections. This was the beginning of my personal relationship with Him, which has grown deeper as the years have passed. It was also the start of finding out about who God is and what He has done.

We read in the Bible that there is only one God.[6] The one God is Father, Son and Holy Spirit. As a human being is only one, yet is body, soul and spirit,[7] so God who made human beings in His own image is Father, Son and Holy Spirit.[8] It is interesting to note that at the very beginning of time God said, 'Let *us* make human beings in *our* image.'[9]

Christians describe God as 'the Trinity': one God who is in three persons, and three persons who are one. Significantly, the Bible, which speaks of the Father, Son and Holy Spirit, ascribes to each attributes that are only God's. From the Bible we also discover many other attributes of His. We learn that God is:

- Spirit.[10] So we must worship Him in spirit and truth.
- Personal.[11] He is interested in each and every one of us.
- Omnipotent, or all-powerful.[12] There is nothing beyond His power.
- Omnipresent, or present everywhere.[13] There is nowhere He cannot be present.
- Omniscient, or all-knowing.[14] There is nothing He cannot know.

- Wise.[15] No one exceeds Him in wisdom.
- Infinite.[16] He has no boundaries.
- Eternal.[17] He has no beginning or end, and lives forever.
- Invisible.[18] He cannot be seen by us.
- Unchangeable or immutable.[19] He does not, and will not, change and so is totally reliable and consistent in all that He says and does.
- Unequalled.[20] No one, including the devil, is His equal in any way whatsoever.
- Holy.[21] He is completely pure and clean, spotless and holy, and to be in His presence is to be overwhelmed with awe.
- Just.[22] He is always fair.
- Patient.[23] He is slow to anger and quick to forgive.
- Merciful, or forgiving.[24] It is part of His nature to show grace, mercy and forgiveness to those who ask Him.
- Angry.[25] God's righteousness is such that with good cause, He is angry over the injustices, ungodliness and unrighteousness in the world.
- Loving.[26] God's very essence is love, and so He is everlastingly loving.
- Everlasting.[27] He has no end, and never becomes weary!
- True.[28] There is no deceit in Him.

And so we could go on! But, perhaps these at present seem distant to you. After all, they are just a list.

Everyone wants to find out why they exist. The three great questions we ask are, 'Where have I come from?', 'What am I doing?' and 'Where am I going?' Modern day fascination with the supernatural not only reveals despair about the state of the present world, but an awareness of another dimension to our existence.

God does not want us to flounder in the dark. He is the one who made us, and has devised means by which we can be brought into a relationship with Him. This is the Christian message. It was summarized by the apostle Paul in the Bible, when he wrote: 'I passed on to you what was most important and what had also been passed on to me. Christ died for our sins, just as the Scriptures said. He was buried, and he was raised from the dead on the third day, just as the Scriptures said.'[29]

Is this the greatest hoax ever to inflict itself on the history of the world? Or, is it in reality God's truth? I trust that reading the chapters of this book will help answer the vital question, why you should believe.

Roger Carswell
Spring 2018

NOTES

1. Genesis 1:1
2. Psalm 14:1
3. Romans 1:20–24
4. John 21:25
5. Acts 1:3, NKJV
6. Deuteronomy 6:4
7. 1 Thessalonians 5:23
8. 1 John 5:7, NKJV
9. Genesis 1:26 (The italics are mine, emphasizing the plurality of personality within the Godhead.)
10. John 4:24
11. John 17:1–3
12. Revelation 19:6
13. Psalm 139:7–12
14. 1 John 3:20

15. Acts 15:18
16. 1 Kings 8:27
17. Isaiah 57:15
18. John 1:18
19. Numbers 23:19
20. Isaiah 40:13–25
21. Revelation 4:8
22. Psalm 89:14
23. Exodus 34:6–7
24. Lamentations 3:22–23
25. Deuteronomy 32:22
26. 1 John 4:8,16
27. Habakkuk 3:6
28. Revelation 15:3
29. 1 Corinthians 15:3–4

1.

Why I Believe the Bible is the Word of God

Jesus said: 'And the very words I have spoken to you are spirit and life.'[1]

For nearly 2,000 years the Bible has been read by millions and has been the greatest influence for good in transforming nations and people. It has also been attacked, burned, banned, insulted and mocked. Today's secular society chooses to give it a wide berth. Although the world's bestseller, in some quarters it is in danger of becoming just another 'classic' – a book which has been heard of by everybody, but nobody has read. In many countries it is a forbidden book: while on the one hand attempting to discredit it, governments sense its power. In some ways, a chapter seeking to prove the Bible to be the Word of God is unnecessary. For if only people would read the Scriptures for themselves they would see them as God's Word carrying its own authenticity and authority.

Consider, for example, the story of a husband, wife and daughter who went to a series of Christian meetings in a village church near Wakefield. They were not Christians, but they were, for the first time, thinking about spiritual issues. At the Wednesday children's meeting, the girl was given a memory verse: 'The wages of sin is death, but the free gift of God is eternal life through Christ Jesus our Lord'. The mother helped her daughter to memorize the verse. As a family they attended each meeting, but gave their apologies for their absence on the Saturday because they were attending a wedding.

After the wedding and reception, some guests went to a local pub for the evening. A comedian was booked to entertain them. One sketch involved him dressing up as a monk and carrying a banner, on which were the words, 'The wages of sin is death.' His derisive mockery was misplaced. God's Word struck to the heart of the woman, who left the pub, went home and trusted Jesus Christ. Her husband asked Jesus into his life the very next day. The truth of God's Word had broken into their world and turned their lives around.

God is not isolated from His creation, denying responsibility for it. He has not left human beings in the lurch. Apart from creation itself, He has revealed Himself to us, through the loving and living Word, Jesus Christ; and through the written Word, the Bible, which itself reveals Christ.

The Bible is human, yet divine

The Bible was written over a period of 1,600 years by about forty authors. Some were heads of state, others subjects; some were lawyers, others labourers; there were conquerors and captives, farmers and fishermen, scholars and shepherds, priests, prophets, poets, and a physician. The Bible tells us about God Himself, and His work in the world. Its scope covers time past, present, future, as well as on into eternity. The Bible is divided into the Old and New Testaments. The Old looks forward to the coming of Christ; the New describes and applies His coming.

The Bible never glosses over the sins or failures of its greatest heroes. We even read of murder, lying, adultery, swearing, pride and bitter contentions in their lives. Every area of life is covered including fear, love, envy, greed, family life, slavery, violence, war and peace, exile, wilderness experiences, life at sea, dreams, songs, wit and music.

The Bible itself claims to be God's message to us. In the Old Testament we read phrases like 'the LORD spoke' or 'thus says the LORD' over two thousand six hundred times. The Bible asserts that:

- All of the Bible is inspired, or God-breathed:
  'All Scripture is inspired by God and is useful to teach us what is true and to make us realise what is wrong in our lives. It corrects us when we are wrong and teaches us to do what is right. God uses it to prepare and equip his people to do every good work.'[2]
- The writers themselves were inspired by God:
  'No prophecy in Scripture ever came from the prophet's own understanding, or from human initiative. No, those prophets were moved by the Holy Spirit, and they spoke from God.'[3]
- Every individual letter is inspired by God:
  The apostle Paul is making a theological point, but uses the Old Testament part of the Bible to give authority to what he is saying, arguing a significant point from just one letter of the alphabet – the difference between the words 'seed' and 'seeds': 'The promises were spoken to Abraham and to his seed. The Scripture does not say "and to seeds", meaning many people, but "and to your seed", meaning one person, who is Christ.'[4]
- Every detail is inspired by God:
  Jesus said, 'I tell you the truth, until heaven and earth disappear, not even the smallest detail of God's law will disappear until its purpose is achieved.'[5]

The clear-cut claim of the Bible is that each of the sixty-six books in their original form – each chapter, each word, and every letter – is given by inspiration of God, and so the Bible is trustworthy and sufficient. It is truly human, yet totally of God.

The Bible is old, yet new

A unique feature of the Bible is its agelessness. This is shown on the one hand by the remarkable recording of future events long before (sometimes hundreds of years before) they happened in history, and on the other by the continual relevancy and application of truths written down centuries ago in a culture that, to us, is quite alien.

Some wish to dismiss the Bible as fable. How, then, do they explain the total accuracy of literally hundreds of prophecies? How was the future so clearly foretold? Who but God, who inhabits eternity, can see what lies ahead? These are not vague predictions such as those of Nostradamus or a fortune-teller's hit-and-miss generalizations, but detailed descriptions of forthcoming events. The statistical improbability of their chance fulfilment is too great to be ignored. Prophecies concerning countries, cities, peoples, individuals, the person and work of Jesus, the progress of the church, the times in which we live, and the end of the world are written in detail throughout the Bible. All, apart from those concerning the end of the world, have been fulfilled in intricate detail. Some, such as the return of the Jews to their own country and the taking again of their capital city, Jerusalem, have happened in comparatively recent years. (Incidentally, it is surely harder to predict the future than to describe the past. If, then, God in His Word accurately foretells the future, can we not trust Him in the accounts of history we read in the Bible?) Repeatedly God, a God of love, warns various groups of people of impending judgement if they do not turn from their wicked ways. These love-based warnings became some of the most amazing fulfilled prophecies; they were fulfilled before watching nations, and so specifically that no one with integrity could deny their authenticity.

Neither the birth of Buddha, Mohammed nor any of the many gurus was predicted; but the birth, life, teaching, work, death, and resurrection of Christ were all carefully prophesied hundreds of years before His incarnation. Who but a timeless God could see the future and cause to have written down so precisely what would happen? Interestingly, of course, the Old Testament is basically a Jewish book, and therefore Christians cannot be open to the charge of 'tampering' with or changing these prophecies. Every Jewish scholar would vouch for the accuracy of the Old Testament Scriptures we shall quote. The Bible remains the world's most translated book as well as the world's bestseller. In the first five books of the Bible alone, phrases such as 'the LORD spoke', 'the LORD commanded' or 'the word of the LORD' occur nearly seven hundred times; in the complete Old Testament, as we have seen, over two thousand six hundred times. The Old Testament saturates the New, which itself fulfils the Old. We shall look at three groups (from the dozens we could have chosen) of these prophecies concerning:

A specific place
In 588 BC the prophet Ezekiel said:

> *Therefore, this is what the Sovereign LORD says: I am your enemy, O Tyre, and I will bring many nations against you, like the waves of the sea crashing against your shoreline. They will destroy the walls of Tyre and tear down its towers. I will scrape away its soil and make it a bare rock! ... This is what the Sovereign LORD says: From the north I will bring King Nebuchadnezzar of Babylon against Tyre. He is king of kings*

23

and brings his horses, chariots, charioteers, and great army. First he will destroy your mainland villages. Then he will attack you by building a siege wall, constructing a ramp, and raising a roof of shields against you … They will plunder all your riches and merchandise and break down your walls. They will destroy your lovely homes and dump your stones and timbers and even your dust into the sea … I will make your island a bare rock, a place for fishermen to spread their nets. You will never be rebuilt, for I, the LORD, have spoken. Yes, the Sovereign LORD has spoken! … I will bring you to a terrible end, and you will exist no more. You will be looked for, but you will never again be found. I, the Sovereign LORD, have spoken![6]

The prediction states that Nebuchadnezzar would destroy the mainland city of Tyre. Many nations would be against the city and eventually make her a flat bare rock; only fishermen would spread nets over the site and debris would be thrown into the water. The city would never be rebuilt and never found again.

Three years after the prophecy, Nebuchadnezzar laid siege to mainland Tyre. As the *Encyclopaedia Britannica* states, 'After a thirteen-year siege (585–573 BC) by Nebuchadnezzar II Tyre made terms and acknowledged Babylonian suzerainty.' However, when Nebuchadnezzar broke down the gates, the city was almost empty. Most of the people had moved by ship to an island about half a mile from the coast, and had fortified a city there. In 573 BC, the mainland city was destroyed.

The island city, however, remained powerful until 332 BC. When the inhabitants refused to surrender to him, Alexander the Great totally demolished the old mainland city and with the debris built a causeway 200 feet wide to reach the island city, which he then captured and sacked. Today the old city of Tyre is a bare, flat rock used only by fishermen to dry their nets; the new city is down the coast from the original site. The biblical prophecy was fulfilled exactly as predicted.

A specific person

The Old Testament contains over three hundred references to Christ's coming. His birth, life, death, resurrection and influences are prophesied in detail.

About 400 BC, Malachi wrote: '"Look! I am sending my messenger, and he will prepare the way before me. Then the Lord you are seeking will suddenly come to his Temple. The messenger of the covenant, whom you look for so eagerly, is surely coming," says the LORD of Heaven's Armies.'[7]

This was fulfilled in the coming of John the Baptist: 'He was in the wilderness and preached that people should be baptized to show that they had repented of their sins and turned to God to be forgiven.'[8]

Isaiah, around 700 BC, prophesied the virgin birth of Jesus: 'All right then, the Lord himself will give you the sign. Look! The virgin will conceive a child! She will give birth to a son and will call him Immanuel (which means "God is with us").'[9]

Matthew describes its fulfilment: 'But he did not have sexual relations with her until her son was born. And Joseph named him Jesus.'[10]

Micah (c. 700 BC) even states the place of Jesus' birth: 'But you, O Bethlehem Ephrathah, are only a small village among all the people of Judah. Yet a ruler of Israel will come from you, one whose origins are from the distant past.'[11]

Isaiah (c. 700 BC) described Jesus and His royal descent: 'For a child is born to us, a son is given to us. The government will rest on his shoulders. And he will be called: Wonderful Counsellor, Mighty God, Everlasting Father, Prince of Peace. His government and its peace will never end. He will rule with fairness and justice from the throne of his ancestor David for all eternity. The passionate commitment of the LORD of Heaven's Armies will make this happen!'[12]

Zechariah (c. 500 BC) describes Jesus' entry into Jerusalem, 'Rejoice, O people of Zion! Shout in triumph, O people of Jerusalem! Look, your king is coming to you. He is righteous and victorious, yet he is humble, riding on a donkey – riding on a donkey's colt.'[13]

We read of Jesus' betrayal, 'Even my best friend, the one I trusted completely, the one who shared my food, has turned against me.'[14]

Written about 1,000 BC and in Zechariah, '"If you like, give me my wages, whatever I am worth; but only if you want to." So they counted out for my wages thirty pieces of silver. And the LORD said to me, "Throw it to the potter" – this magnificent sum at which they valued me! So I took the thirty coins and threw them to the potter in the Temple of the LORD.'[15]

The death of Christ, which is the central theme of the Bible, and is God's means of bringing us to Himself, was prophesied hundreds of years before it happened and indeed before crucifixion was devised. Zechariah wrote in about 500 BC:

> 'Awake, O sword, against my shepherd, the man who is my partner,' says the LORD of Heaven's Armies. 'Strike down the shepherd, and the sheep will be scattered, and I will turn against the lambs.'[16]

> I will pour out a spirit of grace and prayer on the family of David and on the people of Jerusalem. They will look on me whom they have pierced and mourn for him as for an only son. They will grieve bitterly for him as for a firstborn son who has died.[17]

Isaiah (c. 700 BC) graphically wrote concerning the awful events of Christ's crucifixion:

> *But many were amazed when they saw him. His face was so disfigured he seemed hardly human, and from his appearance, one would scarcely know he was a man.*[18]

> *Who has believed our message? To whom has the LORD revealed his powerful arm? My servant grew up in the LORD's presence like a tender green shoot, like a root in dry ground. There was nothing beautiful or majestic about his appearance, nothing to attract us to him. He was despised and rejected – a man of sorrows, acquainted with deepest grief. We turned our backs on him and looked the other way. He was despised, and we did not care. Yet it was our weaknesses he carried; it was our sorrows that weighed him down. And we thought his troubles were a punishment from God, a punishment for his own sins! But he was pierced for our rebellion, crushed for our sins. He was beaten so we could be whole. He was whipped so we could be healed. All of us, like sheep, have strayed away. We have left God's paths to follow our own. Yet the LORD laid on him the sins of us all … He had done no wrong and had never deceived anyone. But he was buried like a criminal; he was put in a rich man's grave. But it was the LORD's good plan to crush him and cause him grief. Yet when his life is made an offering for sin, he will have many descendants. He will enjoy a long life, and the LORD's good plan will prosper in his hands. When he sees all that is accomplished by his anguish, he will be satisfied. And because of his experience, my righteous servant will make it possible for many to be counted righteous, for he will bear all their sins. I will give him the honours of a victorious soldier, because he exposed himself to death. He was counted among the rebels. He bore the sins of many and interceded for rebels.*[19]

David (c. 1,000 BC) described the agony of crucifixion, the gambling for Christ's garments and how no bones of Jesus would be broken:

> My life is poured out like water, and all my bones are out of joint. My heart is like wax, melting within me. My strength has dried up like sunbaked clay. My tongue sticks to the roof of my mouth. You have laid me in the dust and left me for dead. My enemies surround me like a pack of dogs; an evil gang closes in on me. They have pierced my hands and feet. I can count all my bones. My enemies stare at me and gloat. They divide my garments among themselves and throw dice for my clothing.[20]

> For the LORD protects the bones of the righteous; not one of them is broken![21]

> But instead, they give me poison for food; they offer me sour wine for my thirst.[22]

As Dale Rhoton says, 'To the open-minded person the conclusion is inescapable. These prophecies must have come from God and therefore what they said must have been true.'[23]

How does an atheist explain such prophecies? They are clear evidence of the Bible being the Word of God.

A specific people

The Bible says much about the Jewish people. The 'father of the Jews' was Abraham. To him God promised and prophesied the Israelites' 400 years of slavery in Egypt followed by their return to the land He would give them.[24] In the book of Deuteronomy, God warned of the disasters that would come upon the nation of Israel if they deliberately disobeyed his will.[25] He spoke specifically of the Jewish dispersal and persecution. Centuries later the prophet Jeremiah pleaded with God's people to turn from their sins. They continually rejected God's warnings through him. Jeremiah wrote that for seventy years the people would be in captivity in Babylon. This is exactly what eventually happened, in fulfilment of specific prophecies.[26]

The Bible also makes prophecies and predictions that are, in reality, promises concerning God's people today. In each continent and country there are men and women, young and old, who trust and believe in Christ. They are in a real sense God's special people.[27] Knowing Christ proves not just academically but experientially the truth and reality of such statements as:

Is anyone thirsty? Come and drink – even if you have no money! Come, take your choice of wine or milk – it's all free! Why spend your money on food that does not give you strength? Why pay for food that does you no good? Listen to me, and you will eat what is good. You will enjoy the finest food. Come to me with your ears wide open. Listen, and you will find life. I will make an everlasting covenant with you. I will give you all the unfailing love I promised to David.[28]

And I will give you a new heart, and I will put a new spirit in you. I will take out your stony, stubborn heart and give you a tender, responsive heart. And I will put my Spirit in you so that you will follow my decrees and be careful to obey my regulations … I will cleanse you of your filthy behaviour.[29]

The Word gave life to everything that was created, and his life brought light to everyone … But to all who believed him and accepted him, he gave the right to become children of God. They are reborn – not with a physical birth resulting from human passion or plan, but a birth that comes from God ... From his abundance we have all received one gracious blessing after another.[30]

My purpose is to give them a rich and satisfying life.[31]

This means that anyone who belongs to Christ has become a new person. The old life is gone; a new life has begun![32]

At this point, it should be stressed that Christians are not at all anti-science, even though the media often gives this impression. Science is the systematic pursuit of knowledge and, of course, discovering aspects of truth is perfectly consistent with Christian experience. History verifies this, as so many scientists, such as Isaac Newton, Robert Boyle, James Simpson, Michael Faraday, Verna Wright and many, many others were practising Christians.

The problem is that we have cloaked the scientist with a mantle of infallibility, but a true scientist is known by their confession of ignorance. For example, Johannes Kepler, who discovered that planetary orbits are elliptical, reflected, 'O God, I am thinking Thy thoughts after Thee.' Isaac Newton said: 'I do not know what I may appear to the world, but to myself I seem to have been only like a boy playing on the sea-shore, and diverting myself in now and then finding a smoother pebble or a prettier shell than ordinary, whilst the great ocean of truth lay all undiscovered before me.'

The inventor Thomas Edison once stated, 'I do not know one millionth part of one per cent about anything.'

Edward Jenner, the discoverer of the benefits of vaccination, said, 'I do not wonder that men are grateful to me, but I am surprised that they do not feel gratitude to God for thus making me a medium of good.'

After all, scientists cannot explain the source of kindness, love, beauty, friendship or fairness. They cannot say where we are going, or why it is that humankind universally demonstrates a spiritual dimension and a desire to worship.

However, the question, 'Why believe, when we have science?' is still a common sentiment of many. The notion that the first book of the Bible, Genesis, is to be discarded as myth is popular dogma.

The book of Genesis is arguably the most important book ever to be written. It is the foundation to the world's bestseller, the Bible. It is the basis of the most influential piece of literature to have been produced. If the first thirty-four verses of Genesis are true, then atheism, agnosticism, materialism, hedonism, existentialism, polytheism and pantheism are all invalidated. If Genesis is true, our most pressing need is to find out more about the Creator God who made us and to whom we are responsible.

True science does not contradict the Bible, nor does the Bible contradict true science. There are, however, scientific theories (rather than proven facts) and misguided biblical interpretations that may give the impression that there are contradictions. Perhaps limited knowledge leads to limited theories upon which many feel they can build a case and a life that excuses them from trust in God.

Take, for example, the two areas of controversy relating to the creation of the world and miraculous acts. Theories seeking to describe scientifically the age of the world and how it began are often thought to prove the Bible to be untrue. However, there are other explanations.

Some have suggested that perhaps the six days of creation in Genesis 1 really represent long periods of time. 'After all,' they argue, 'are not 1,000 years as a day in the sight of God?'

However, Genesis is a historical rather than a poetical book. Why then should this part alone be interpreted as symbolic?

In Genesis 1 we read of the chronological order of creation, then in chapter 2, humans are the focal point of attention and the centre point of creation. All creation is seen in relation to the pinnacle of creation.

Adam and Eve were made with 'apparent age'. They were not created as little babies, but rather as adults. Interestingly, the plants, trees, fish and animals were likewise made with the physical appearance of maturity. There has been much questioning about the age of the earth. Perhaps it was made with apparent age too?

In the early chapters of Genesis we read of the origin of the universe, of order, of the solar system, of the atmosphere and hydrosphere, of life, of humans, of marriage, of evil, of language, of government, of culture, of nations, of religion, of music, of poetry, of communities and of a chosen people.

If we truly grasped the greatness of the 'God-ness' of God, our question would not be, 'How could God create such a complex world in such a short time?', but 'Why did He take six days creating something that could have been made in an instant?'

In all the world there is the seal of a great and amazing Creator of such marvellous things. I once saw a cartoon that expresses the wonder of the beauty of creation. It showed two monks surveying some beautiful scenery in the distance. One was saying to the other, 'I like his use of green in the bottom left-hand corner!' Nature testifies to the glory of God. It is reasonable to believe that behind designs there must be a Designer, behind something made there must be a Maker, behind creation there must be a Creator.

But the sceptic will also question the miracles. Again, though, if God is truly God, He is well able to intervene, even if the result does not act in accordance with the usual observable laws of nature. Here is the clue to overcoming what has been a problem to some. A scientist is limited in being able only to explain what he actually sees. If God is taken into account, the explanation and outcome may be very different.

For example, given a piece of bread and asked to describe how it was made, a scientist would naturally detail how the corn was planted in the earth, its growth, harvesting, grinding, mixing with other ingredients, and finally its baking in the oven. Of course, that would be fine, unless, that is, something remarkably exceptional had happened. Suppose, instead, the particular piece of bread under examination was one that had been picked up after Jesus had taken five loaves and two fishes, given thanks, then broken and distributed them to feed the 5,000.[33] We read that twelve baskets of leftovers were gathered. If the piece of bread in question was one of these fragments, or from the incident a little later when Jesus fed 4,000 with seven loaves and a few fish,[34] the scientist would have been wrong in his analysis and description, because he failed to take into account the supernatural hand of God.

The scientist would make a similar and understandable mistake if he or she described the birth, growth, catching and grilling of the fish, if in fact this too was the product of miraculous and instantaneous multiplication by Jesus. Or again, suppose wine were given to a professional wine-taster or a scientist to describe its country of origin and vintage. As they swilled it round in the glass, smelled and tasted it, they could perhaps describe this mature-tasting drink, perhaps even locating its country of origin and pinpointing one of the finest vineyards in that land. However, this time, far from being the natural product of grapes that had undergone years of fermentation, it was made in an instant. Jesus was attending a wedding feast at Cana in Galilee.[34] The wine ran out, but Jesus commanded that six large earthenware pots be filled with water. As the chief steward tasted the drink, he found it was the best of wine. Knowledge of the presence of the one who created it would change the whole outlook on the wine itself. It was made in an instant rather than the long process that appeared to be the more obvious method.

If the Bible is as it claims to be, the Word of God, then we would expect to read of the works of God. If these were within the realm of normal human experience, then one would rightly question whether they were a demonstration of God or merely of humans. It is surely reasonable to expect God to work in ways that are beyond human comprehension. This does not disprove the Bible, but demonstrates the infinite power of God and the limitations of our finite minds and scientific pursuit.

The Bible is a library, yet one book

Most books are the product of an individual author. The Bible, in contrast, was written by more than forty authors over sixteen centuries. They came from four cultures and wrote in three languages (Hebrew, Aramaic and Greek) on three continents. For example, the old man Moses wrote in the wilderness in Hebrew 1,500 years before the apostle John, incarcerated in prison on the isle of Patmos, wrote his book of the Revelation, in Greek. It doesn't matter whether the authors produced their writings in a nomadic tent, a beautiful palace, a dungeon, in the midst of battle, or out in the fields. Each sentence is part of an overall picture that is united and complete. History, poetry, prophecy, letters and gospel records combine to form a revelation that is a perfect blueprint from God to us.

One would expect a clash of culture, thought, philosophy and belief; however, there is absolute harmony. Doctrines, outlook and even the use of words blend together perfectly.

Unity in doctrine

As soon as Adam and Eve sinned, they are seen hiding from God, who took the initiative in searching for them. Whereas most other major world religions are alike in that they are all to do with humanity struggling to find a way back to God, biblical religion is unique; it is about God coming to seek and to save us, who are lost. The theme of the Bible is redemption (God buying back errant, lost people). In the Old Testament it is foretold and pictured; in the New it is accomplished and applied.

Think for a moment of this volume written over a period of 1,600 hundred years by forty different men, but consistently speaking so eloquently of the holiness of God, the wrongdoing of men and women, the redemption Christ died to buy for us, as well as the promise of spiritual life on earth and in eternity for those who by faith come to know God. Without collaboration, these authors were 'of a mind' as they wrote of God's dealings with them.

What do I do if I recognize my wrongdoing and guilt, longing for it to be removed? Am I really to believe that visiting Mecca, Rome, the River Ganges or some other 'holy' place is sufficient to please God? Will turning over a new leaf and seeking not to err again make up for my past deficiencies? Does God merely desire that I become an automaton, submissive to my religious rituals? The Bible teaches another and better way altogether.

Sin always brings death: either the death of the sinner, or the death of a sacrifice or substitute. In Old Testament days, God ordained that a sinner was to take a spotless male lamb to the Jewish priest. This was in itself an act of confession. The sinner and the Jewish priest would lay a hand on the head of the lamb. Then the lamb would die, its blood shed for sin. Thousands upon thousands died in this way, not because God loves bloodshed, but to reveal the horrible seriousness of sin, and to portray God's ultimate remedy for it in Christ.

The shadowy picture of animal sacrifice in the Old Testament was eventually to be done away with completely. In the fullness of time, a baby was born. The angel said, 'call His name JESUS, for he will save His people from their sins.'[36] There was only one way He could do that; He was to die as a sacrifice and a substitute for the world's sin. No wonder when John the Baptist saw Jesus, he pointed the crowds to Him saying, 'Look! The Lamb of God who takes away the sin of the world!'[37]

Jesus was to die as the innocent, pure, male lamb. He took away that which no animal could take. He carried on Himself all past and future wrongs. He was completing what Jewish writers and readers had eagerly looked for over many centuries. No wonder He was to cry on the cross, 'It is finished.' He was speaking of this completed work of redemption.

Paul wrote that 'he purchased our freedom with the blood of his Son' and Peter said 'the ransom he paid was not mere gold or silver. It was the precious blood of Christ, the sinless, spotless Lamb of God.'[38] The very last book in the Bible foretells a theme in heaven for all those who have trusted in the finished work of Christ: 'Worthy is the Lamb who was slaughtered'.[39]

The themes of the universal nature of sin and its seriousness, as well as the necessity of being redeemed by the Lamb of God, are examples of the continuity of theme that exists throughout the Bible.

Unity in outlook
Using imagery, symbolism, logic, oratory, poetry and reasoning, there is a spiritual tone throughout the Bible that describes the pathos and trauma of a godless society that is set on rejecting God and His commands; yet it produces profound hope solidly based on the work and promises of God. For example:

Day and night I have only tears for food, while my enemies continually taunt me, saying, 'Where is this God of yours?' ...

*Why am I discouraged? Why is my heart so sad? I will put my
hope in God! I will praise him again – my Saviour and my God!*[40]

Moses, 500 years before the psalm was written, and the disciples,
1,000 years after, had the same attitude; namely, a deep pessimism
at the sinfulness of people overtaken by total optimism, knowing
the overriding and triumphant power of God's goodness.

Unity in words

Bible scholars have long been aware of the miraculous unity
in the Word of God, and hence have often studied individual
words and their use throughout the Bible. As with the doctrines,
there are many examples, but here let us take the example of
the word 'thorns'.

God cursed the earth after we had first sinned. The Lord said,
'It will grow thorns and thistles for you, though you will eat of
its grains.'[41] So thorns are the result of wrongdoing and the curse
of God.

Later, when Abraham was stopped from sacrificing his son
Isaac, God told him instead to sacrifice a ram caught in a thicket,
or thorn bush.[42] The sacrifice was caught by that which represents
sin – the thorns.

When Jesus Christ was to be crucified, He had wedged on
His head a crown made with thorns. The mark of sin was now
crowning the one who would save the world. After all, that is
what the cross was all about.

Although the Bible is a collection of books, it is actually one book
with one theme revealing the one and only way to the one God.

The Bible is ignored, yet influential

Although the Bible is widely distributed and easily available in the
West, it is a characteristic of recent generations in some countries,

especially in Europe, that through the media and educational systems, they are ignoring or attacking it.

Most people feel they have a smattering of knowledge, but in reality this is limited. Religious cults capitalize on this by quoting verses selectively, thus giving the impression that they know their Bible. Some who go to church have little real grasp of biblical truths and fail to allow their lives to be governed by them.

The Bible has been read by more people and translated into more languages than any other book. It has survived through time, persecution and criticism as the anvil upon which many hammers have had their day but been eventually discarded as ineffective. For example, Tom Paine wrote one of the first anti-Bible books, entitled *The Age of Reason*. He concludes with words to this effect, 'I have been through the Bible like a woodman going through trees with his axe. Let the priests try and put the trees back on the stumps if they can.'[43] This was written, of course, many years ago. Tom Paine is dead and forgotten; yet the Bible not only lives but goes forward with growing influence. The 'priests' did not put the trees back on their stumps; the trees were never severed. Tom Paine was wrong.

In 1874, the Scriptures were under severe attack by critics, and John W. Haley published a defence entitled *Alleged Discrepancies of the Bible*. In the preface he wrote:

> *Finally, let it be remembered that the Bible is neither dependent upon nor affected by the success or failure of my book. Whatever may become of the latter, whatever may be the verdict passed upon it by an intelligent public, the Bible will stand. In the ages yet to be, when its present assailants and defenders are mouldering in the dust, and when our very names are forgotten, [God's Word] will be, as it has been during the centuries past, the guide and solace of millions.*[44]

My experience is that those who attack Scripture most are those who know it least. Those who accuse it of being full of contradictions have picked up second-hand arguments and not checked to find the straightforward answers that are in the context of the passage.

Gladstone, the illustrious nineteenth-century prime minister, wrote a book on the Bible entitled *The Impregnable Rock of Holy Scripture*. When Churchill read it, he commented that he had no reason to disagree. Such men are not hoodwinked, nor are the millions who have staked their lives and eternities upon its teachings and promises.

The Bible may be ignored by many, but its power is unleashed upon those who read it.

A Yorkshire miner was converted after reading the words: 'For God so loved the world that he gave his only begotten Son' on the back of a bus ticket. Presumably the next part of the famous verse found in John 3:16 was on the next bus ticket! A London journalist trusted Christ after reading the words 'Christ died for our sins' imprinted on a cheap Biro. Neither of these individuals had any religious background, but God's Word, the Bible, spoke powerfully to them both.

Professor Michael Clarkson heads up the Department of Veterinary Parasitology at Liverpool University. He was brought up as an atheist, and as he started his studies he would have described himself as agnostic. Intrigued by the title of a lecture being organized by Christians at the university, he went to listen to a clergyman speak on 'The Impossibility of Agnosticism'. He was not convinced, but took up the challenge of the speaker, who said he would give a booklet to anyone who wanted one, which he guaranteed would lead to the conversion of anybody reading it with an open mind. Sceptically, Michael Clarkson took a copy – it was John's gospel. Carefully he read it. In the silence of his home, he became convinced of its truths and believed God, trusted and followed Jesus.

The Bible's influence is second to none. Adolf Hitler wrote in the preface to *Mein Kampf*: 'I know that fewer people are won over by the written word than by the spoken word and that every great movement on this earth owes its growth to great speakers and not to great writers.'[45] As far as the Bible is concerned, Hitler was wrong. When a person starts to read, God's power is shown, as the Holy Spirit takes hold of the Bible and powerfully applies it to transform lives.

In both the joys and deepest struggles of life, the Bible has been a source of inward strength to many.

If Alexander Graham Bell was the improver of the telephone, Philipp Reis, was its inventor. At the end of his life, he referred to the 'Holy Scriptures' saying, 'The Lord has bestowed more good upon me than I have known how to ask of him. The Lord has helped me hitherto; he will help yet further.'

William Wilberforce, whose labours brought about the abolition of slavery in the British Empire, wrote: 'My judgement … rests altogether on the word of God' and 'If you read the Scriptures with earnest prayer … and a sincere desire for discovering the truth and obeying it when known, I cannot doubt of your attaining it.'

Woodrow Wilson, the US statesman and president said, 'When you have read the Bible, you will know that it is the Word of God, because you will have found it the key to your own heart, your own happiness and your own duty.'

The great nineteenth-century American preacher, Henry Ward Beecher wrote, 'The Bible is God's chart for you to steer by, to keep you from the bottom of the sea, and to show you where the harbour is and how to reach it without running on rocks or bars.'

Bible translators continue their relentless task of translating the Scriptures into every language, because they know the power of the Word of God to change and improve not only individuals, but culture and behaviour. The Bible gives the one remedy to the trap of guilt and sin.

Our own culture has been permeated by the truths of the Bible, truths that have affected our democracy, our legal system, our freedoms, our arts, music, literature, and architecture. Such is the influence of the Bible.

I have read the Bible, yet the Bible read me

I don't know that I would have read a 170-page biography of a Middle Eastern pastor who lived during the first part of the twentieth century – except that my mother wrote it. I not only read it, but loved it. Knowing the author made all the difference.

The Bible is not like a Shakespearian play, intended to be read merely as literature. Rather, it is a book that is spiritually understood. It has a divine author, one who is reaching out in love to lost men and women. Through its words, God speaks. Praying and asking God to teach us as we read is the way to benefit from the Word of God.

As you read, you discover that God sees us just as we are. So many won't read it because they know they are guilty of the wrongdoing it condemns. The Bible condemns every sin and condones none; it accuses all and excuses none; it abuses human reason and exalts God's revelation. It points us away from ourselves to Christ. It is the Word of God and therefore ought to be read daily until it becomes a delight. Why not read it yourself? Start in the New Testament, say with Luke's gospel. Don't use notes or commentaries, but just let God Himself teach you as you read.

NOTES

1. John 6:63
2. 2 Timothy 3:16–17
3. 2 Peter 1:20–21
4. Galatians 3:16, NIV
5. Matthew 5:18
6. Ezekiel 26:3–4,7–8,12,14,21
7. Malachi 3:1
8. Mark 1:4
9. Isaiah 7:14
10. Matthew 1:25
11. Micah 5:2
12. Isaiah 9:6–7
13. Zechariah 9:9
14. Psalm 41:9
15. Zechariah 11:12–13
16. Zechariah 13:7
17. Zechariah 12:10
18. Isaiah 52:14
19. Isaiah 53:1–6,9–12
20. Psalm 22:14–18
21. Psalm 34:20
22. Psalm 69:21
23. Dale Rhoton, *The Logic of Faith* (Bromley: STL Books, 1978), p.72
24. Genesis 15:12–16
25. Deuteronomy 28:15 ff.
26. Jeremiah 29:10 ff.; Daniel 9:2
27. 1 Peter 2:9
28. Isaiah 55:1–3
29. Ezekiel 36:26–27,29
30. John 1:4,12–13,16

31. John 10:10
32. 2 Corinthians 5:17
33. Interestingly, this miracle appears in each of the four Gospels, Matthew, Mark, Luke and John
34. Matthew 15:32–39
35. John 2:1–11
36. Matthew 1:21, NKJV
37. John 1:29
38. Ephesians 1:7; 1 Peter 1:18–19
39. Revelation 5:12
40. Psalm 42:3,11
41. Genesis 3:18
42. Genesis 22:13
43. Thomas Paine, *The Age of Reason* (New York: Citadel, 2000)
44. John W. Haley, *Alleged Discrepancies of the Bible* (New Kensington, PA: Whitaker House, 1984)
45. Adolf Hitler, *Mein Kampf* (Mumbai, India: Jaico Publishing House; 37th Jaico Impression 2007 edition, 2007)

2.

Why I Believe the Devil is the Enemy of God

Jesus said: 'I don't have much more time to talk to you, because the ruler of this world approaches. He has no power over me ... take heart, because I have overcome the world.'[1]

A friend of mine was visiting a Church Missionary Society hospital in Kenya. While being taken round and introduced to some of the patients, he met an African whose arms were just bandaged stumps. Enquiring about what had happened, he was told that the patient was a village witchdoctor. His power was such that if anyone crossed him, he would simply point at his enemy, and before the day was over they would be dead. The villagers had been in such fear of the witchdoctor's power that one night they banded together, raided his hut, chopped off his hands so he could never again point, and took him to the missionary hospital. Although they took drastic measures against the witchdoctor, they knew well enough the reality of Satan's power.

The devil is not the red man carrying a pitchfork, seeking to do little bits of mischief wherever he can, as often caricatured by the cartoonist. Neither is he the all-powerful undefeatable foe that some see him as. We shall see later in this chapter that Jesus has already won the victory over Satan by His work on the cross.[2] It is also true that God gives Christians weapons not only to resist Satan, but to send him running.[3]

The Bible says two things about everything that is associated with the devil, be it sorcery, fortune telling, astrology, spiritualism, the occult or powers of darkness: first, they are real and are to be taken seriously, and second, they are wrong, hated by God and therefore to be avoided. The Bible records the disastrous consequences of those who choose to ignore God's commands concerning Satan.

The career of the first king of Israel, King Saul, started well, but he ended his days by consulting a medium. Earlier he had ordered that the land be cleared of such people, but eventually he was to ask, 'I have to talk to a man who has died ... Will you call up his spirit for me?'[4] His contact with the witch of Endor was as a direct result of his separation from God.[5] A few days later, Saul was to die in battle.

Centuries later, Isaiah had to contend with a whole nation that was set on seeking mediums and wizards.[6] Eventually the nation, having turned its back on God, was overrun by enemy armies.

In more recent years, interest in the occult has been greater than one at first might imagine. Peter Anderson in his book *Talk of the Devil* mentions some of the more influential characters who have had such involvement:

> *Mary Baker Eddy, founder of Christian Science, worked as a professional medium in New York for many years. Joseph Smith, originator of the Mormon religion, claims to have received his 'revelations' from a spirit that he knew as 'Moroni'. Emmanuel Swedenborg, whose followers founded the churches of the 'New*

Jerusalem', claimed to have communicated with the 'dead' on many occasions.

Dr Carl Jung, the famous Swiss psychologist, also possessed unusual occult powers and often had horoscopes cast for his patients. He claimed to have a spirit guide named 'Philemon', and often spoke with him. In fact, Dr Jung won his doctorate with a thesis on the subject of the occult.

Abraham Lincoln consulted with a medium over his 'Emancipation Proclamation'. Jeane Dixon, the American clairvoyant, claims that on more than one occasion President Roosevelt invited her to predict for him. Even Sir Winston Churchill said that there had been times when he had turned to the 'spirit of the glass' for help in his hour of need.

Astrologers were engaged by several governments during World War Two and many of these produced astrological calculations for propaganda purposes. In Nazi Germany, Himmler employed a corps of mediums in the service of the SS.

British mediums have on occasions offered their services to the police, and one well known Dutch clairvoyant has been consulted by at least seven European police chiefs in murder investigations.[7]

In addition Richard Wurmbrand, the Romanian pastor who was imprisoned for his faith in Christ during the Communist years, has argued that Marx was in fact a Satanist.[8]

Today in our secular society, well-known book clubs promote authors and books that revel in the supernatural; high street bookshops sell tarot cards; toy shops sell games such as 'Dungeons and Dragons', 'Horoscope', 'Mystic Eye', and Ouija boards; cinemas and television repeatedly show films about the supernatural with its sadism, sordidness and sensuality. Horoscopes appear in newspapers, magazines, television and radio programmes, and on apps. They are in the thinking of the general public. Mediums fill town halls, pubs and seaside theatres as they publicly conduct séances and tell fortunes, and famous entertainers encourage their followers to emulate them by publicly sharing their involvement in the occult.

For Christians this is sad, but not surprising. The apostle Paul said that a sign of 'the last times' would be people departing 'from the true faith; they will follow deceptive spirits and teachings that come from demons'.[9]

Who then is the devil?

The Bible describes the devil as a spiritual being who has intelligence, power and authority. He is the source of all that is evil. That does not mean that we are not responsible for our actions. 'The devil made me do it' is no excuse – we are the ones who did it!

In the Bible he is called the angel of death, a liar and the father of lies, the deceiver, a murderer, the commander of the powers in the unseen world, and the serpent.[10] He is likened to a roaring lion seeking people to devour.[11] He (and not 'leisure, pleasure or treasure') is called 'the god of this world'.[12]

Jesus likened the devil to a thief who comes to steal, to kill and to destroy.[13] Destructive forces in Christian work and divisive influences in churches are surely inspired by the devil. Suicidal thoughts could well be triggered by Satan, though of course, some suffer in this way through illness of the mind. Certainly Satan attacks Christians and buffets them. He is described as hindering Christian work, as Paul found when he desired to visit the believers in Thessalonica.[14] The original word, written in Greek, rendered 'hindered' in this verse, literally means 'to break up the road along the way'.

Jesus warned that in the last days Satan would perform signs and wonders – even 'signs and lying wonders'. In fact, although

Jesus Himself performed signs, He often warned against Satan's counterfeiting of them.[15]

If there is no devil, who inspired Adolf Hitler to systematically exterminate the Jews, and bring about suffering for millions? Who was behind a terrorist who packed explosives over his body then drove a lorry full of explosives into an American camp in Beirut, killing himself and 100 marines? Who inspired the 9/11 bombers to fly hijacked planes into the Twin Towers in New York, killing themselves and over two thousand others? Who has brought the world to the brink of self-destruction? Who was behind what people described as 'an outburst of evil' in the riots in London in August 2011? Who has led millions to ignore God and live with no thought of Him?

God is a Trinity – there is a plurality of persons in the Godhead – the Father, the Son and the Holy Spirit. The devil is the enemy of each member of the Trinity.

The devil – the enemy of the Father

We do not know all the details of the early work and fall of the devil. However, he was obviously a beautiful, created angel who wanted to be as God. Isaiah fills in some detail:

> *How you are fallen from heaven, O shining star, son of the morning! You have been thrown down to the earth, you who destroyed the nations of the world. For you said to yourself, 'I will ascend to heaven and set my throne above God's stars. I will preside on the mountain of the gods far away in the north. I will climb to the highest heavens and be like the Most High.' Instead, you will be brought down to the place of the dead, down to its lowest depths.*[16]

Pride filled the devil. As we see from this Bible passage, he said 'I will' three times, rather than 'Your will be done', which were the words of Jesus in His prayer before going to His crucifixion.

Having been thrown out of heaven to the hell prepared for him and his angels, the devil then set to work to destroy the wonder of creation. He approached Adam and Eve questioning the word of God, adding to it, taking from it and changing it (a pattern of operation the devil still follows today). The devil sought to substitute a lie for the truth of God's word. All that radiated the glory of God, the devil tried to tarnish. Adam and Eve lost their purity, perfection and paradise when they followed the temptation of Satan

It is thought that the oldest book in the Bible is Job. It tells the story of a godly man whose family and business were blessed of God. The devil, the supreme cynic, attributed wrong motives to Job's apparent godliness saying:

> *Yes, but Job has good reason to fear God. You have always put a wall of protection around him and his home and his property. You have made him prosper in everything he does. Look how rich he is! But reach out and take away everything he has, and he will surely curse you to your face!*[17]

In a matter of days, Job had lost all his ten children, his business and his health. The devil's prediction was wrong – Job did not curse God.

The devil may be the enemy of the Father, but the Father has deposed him. We read: 'For God did not spare even the angels who sinned. He threw them into hell, in gloomy pits of darkness, where they are being held until the day of judgment.'[18] God can only ever do one thing with sin or the source of sin – that is, to remove it from His presence. In deposing the devil, the Father has cut off and cast from Him the offending angels for ever.

The devil – the enemy of the Son

It had long been in the plan of God that He should send His dear Son to accomplish the work of dying to save men and women.[19] Employing a four-point strategy, the devil did his utmost to keep Jesus from coming and carrying out His purpose.

To prevent Jesus coming to earth

When Egypt was on the crest of a wave, it had the whole nation of Israel as slaves building and working for it. Suddenly, without provocation, the king of Egypt spoke to the midwives and said: 'When you help the Hebrew women as they give birth … If the baby is a boy, kill him.'[20] This was economic suicide and completely irrational. The intention was clear; to exterminate the Israelite nation forever. If that had been done, Christ could not have come to the earth.

The devil attempted to destroy Israel a second time. In about 475 BC the Persian king Ahasuerus (or Xerxes) reigned over 127 provinces from India to Ethiopia. Haman, the king's right-hand man, approached Ahasuerus and said: 'There is a certain race of people scattered through all the provinces of your empire … If it please the king, issue a decree that they be destroyed'. Permission was given: 'The money and the people are both yours to do with as you see fit.'[21]

Both times the plots were thwarted. Each time the ancestral line, which was to lead to Jesus' birth, was protected. The devil's scheme was hindered.

To prevent Jesus living on earth

Shortly after the birth of Jesus in Bethlehem, wise men came from the east asking Herod as to the whereabouts of a baby born to be king. In his anger, Herod ordered the death of all baby boys under the age of 2 in Bethlehem.[22] The intention again was to prevent Jesus from saving men and women. Once more the devil was defeated and Jesus lived.

Repeatedly throughout the life of Jesus, Satan sought to kill Him and stirred up the minds and motives of evil men. When Christ read the Scriptures in the synagogue in Nazareth, the locals rose up in arms against Him, and would have pushed Him off a cliff if Jesus had not passed through the crowd.[23] When Jesus was explaining His deity – that He was Jehovah, God in the flesh – the Jews were so angry they picked up stones to stone Him to death, but Jesus hid and escaped through the Temple.[24] Even the winds and waves seemed to be under the control of the devil when Jesus was asleep in a boat on the Sea of Galilee. Experienced fishermen feared that they would perish in the water, and so woke up Jesus in panic. Jesus stilled the storm and so again the devil's intention to destroy Him came to nothing.[25]

To prevent Jesus living sinlessly on earth

At the start of his three-year ministry, Jesus was baptized by His cousin John, then went into the wilderness for forty days. He prayed, fasted, meditated on the (Old Testament) Scriptures and was tempted. The devil appealed to Jesus physically, suggesting to Him, when He had not eaten for forty days, to 'turn these stones into bread'. Afterwards the devil tempted the soul of Christ, saying 'throw yourself down [from the temple]', so that Jesus would receive immediate acclaim; later Satan attacked Jesus spiritually saying he would give Jesus authority over this world at that moment, if He would bow and worship Satan. Interestingly, the devil tempted Christ in different places – first in the wilderness (symbolizing the place of difficulty and hardship), secondly in the holy city (symbolizing the place of duty, both secular and spiritual), and thirdly, on a high mountain (symbolizing the place of devotion).[26] If Jesus had fallen to any of these repeated temptations, His ministry would have been useless. If Jesus had sinned in any way, He could not have died paying for the sin of the world. He was the only individual whom the devil could not trap.

Satan dogged the footsteps of Jesus throughout the three years of ministry. Judas Iscariot, one of the twelve disciples, was referred to by Christ as 'a devil'.[27] Yet nothing the devil did could make Jesus commit sin.

To prevent Jesus paying the penalty for sin

We do not know how much the devil knew of or understood the plan of God in sending Christ to atone for the world's sin. However, it appears that Satan inspired the people who gathered round Jesus' cross shouting at Him, 'He saved others, but he can't save himself! So he is the King of Israel, is he? Let him come down from the cross right now, and we will believe in him!'[28] Did the thought pass through Jesus' mind, 'They will believe Me if I come down'? Certainly the devil subtly sought to spoil the great work of Christ. Jesus did save others, and to be able to save us, He knew that He must not save Himself.

The devil utterly failed in preventing Jesus coming to this earth and ultimately atoning for sin and rising from the dead.

Jesus finished the work He had come to do. A way for forgiveness of sin has been made. Jesus can bring us to God. But more has been achieved.

The enemy of Jesus has been destroyed. The Father deposed the devil, but Jesus has destroyed his work, and ultimately Satan himself. This is what the Bible says:

> *But the Son of God came to destroy the works of the devil.*[29]

> *Because God's children are human beings – made of flesh and blood – the Son also became flesh and blood. For only as a*

human being could he die, and only by dying could he break the
power of the devil, who had the power of death.[30]

The American writer Warren Wiersbe, in his Bible commentary says:

> *Destroy does not mean 'annihilate'. Satan is certainly still*
> *at work today! 'Destroy' here, means 'to render inoperative, to*
> *rob of power'. Satan has not been annihilated, but his power has*
> *been reduced and his weapons have been impaired. He is still a*
> *mighty foe, but he is no match for the power of God.*[31]

At great cost, Christ has taken the weapons of sin and death from the hand of the devil and driven them into his heart, destroying his power for ever.

The devil – the enemy of the Holy Spirit

The Holy Spirit is God Himself, at work in today's world. Jesus said of the Spirit:

> *And when he comes, he will convict the world of its sin,*
> *and of God's righteousness, and of the coming judgment. The*
> *world's sin is that it refuses to believe in me. Righteousness is*
> *available because I go to the Father, and you will see me no more.*
> *Judgment will come because the ruler of this world has already*
> *been judged.*[32]

If you have ever been driving and looked in your mirror to see the flashing lights of a police car beckoning you to pull over, you will know how rapidly thoughts of self-examination flash through your mind – 'Is my indicator working? Are my tyres all right? Was I speeding?' When God begins to work in a life, He convicts people in a similar way. Suddenly they become intensely aware of their own sin. Whereas previously they had thought themselves to be all right, they become conscious of deep sinfulness. Like a plague or a cancer within, wrongdoing seems to have permeated all parts of their being. Nothing anyone says comforts them. It is the beginning of a period similar to gestation. God uses it to drive those people, whom He loves, to Christ.

However, the devil, the enemy of the Holy Spirit, fills our minds with a host of excuses. It is as if Satan whispers, 'You can't help it ... It's your upbringing ... It's just the way you are ... Everyone else does it.' There is no doubt that many factors such as family, environment, education and personality affect our actions and attitudes. However, the Bible clearly teaches that 'everyone has sinned; we all fall short of God's glorious standard.'[33] The nineteenth-century Scottish preacher Robert Murray McCheyne expressed this same thought when he said in his Victorian English: 'When He has cast light into the sinner's bosom and let him see how every action of his life condemns him, and how vain it is to seek for any righteousness there, He then casts light upon the risen Saviour and says "Look here".'

The Holy Spirit does not leave a person merely conscious of his or her own guilt before God; He then points the person's attention to Jesus. He was completely pure. It was He who took the weight of the world's wrongdoing on Himself on the cross. He died taking the judgement of God against sin on Himself. For the person who believes in Christ, eternal life is guaranteed. The Bible, God's Word, repeatedly promises this. For example:

> *For God so loved the world that He gave His only begotten Son, that whoever believes in Him should not perish but have everlasting life. For God did not send His Son into the world to condemn the world, but that the world through Him might*

be saved. He who believes in Him is not condemned ... Most assuredly, I say to you, he who hears My word and believes in Him who sent Me has everlasting life, and shall not come into judgment, but has passed from death to life.[34]

The Bible clearly teaches that heaven is not a reward; it is a gift. Once again, the argument of the devil is to counter this. He would want to say that Jesus was merely a great religious leader who came to an unfortunate end. Reading of the life of Christ will quickly reveal how untrue this idea is. Jesus Himself said, 'The Son of Man is going to be betrayed into the hands of his enemies. He will be killed, but on the third day he will be raised from the dead'[35] and 'the Son of Man came ... to give his life as a ransom for many'.[36] Jesus is Lord and Saviour.

The devil is the enemy of the work of the Holy Spirit, whose work it is to take the gaze of people from themselves to Jesus.[37] However, the Holy Spirit defeats the devil.

As soon as a person trusts Jesus, they receive forgiveness, God works a miracle; that person is transformed within. Jesus called Christian conversion being 'born again'[38] and Paul described it as being a 'new person'.[39]

So when any person is converted, the Holy Spirit completely transforms that individual, taking them from captivity to liberty, from spiritual death to spiritual life, and from darkness to light.[40]

Broken families and marred relationships have been mended as God, by His Holy Spirit, takes over a situation. Of course, a Christian still experiences problems. The Christian life is a spiritual warfare: followers of Jesus are swimming against the tide of popular society, but God gives Christ's strength to all who belong to Him so they are able to withstand the devil's pressures.

The devil – the enemy of us

As well as being the enemy of God, the devil also hates all human beings. Each individual was made in the image of God, no matter how marred they are now. God loves us and appeals for our trust. The devil seeks to destroy all that is of God, in each person.

The Bible outlines three steps to take to overcome the devil:

Repent

To repent is to be willing to renounce all known wrong. It is not so much an act of the emotions, but of the will. It is taking God's side against our sin. Specifically, it means that the alcoholic, relying on God's strength, will live soberly; the thief will strive to live honestly; the immoral person will be passionate about purity; the gossip will speak kindly; the godless person will want to live a godly life in Jesus.

The great believer, the apostle Paul, who is an example to all Christians, visited Ephesus in his missionary travels. A remarkable work of Christian conversion was done in many people's lives there. Demonstrating their genuine repentance we read of the Ephesian Christians, that 'A number of them who had been practicing sorcery brought their incantation books and burned them at a public bonfire. The value of the books was several million dollars.'[41]

Turning one's back on the devil is a deliberate act of renouncing all the hidden works of darkness. It may mean burning books, whether supernatural or immoral; destroying music whose symbols and themes are taken up with the devil, superstition, the occult or hell; and disposing of games that create interest in the occult.

Receive Christ

Having turned from one's past life, it is important not to leave a vacuum, but rather to turn to Jesus. He warned against merely making moral adjustments without true repentance and genuine faith.

> *When an evil spirit leaves a person, it goes into the desert, searching for rest. But when it finds none, it says, 'I will return to the person I came from.' So it returns and finds that its former home is all swept and in order. Then the spirit finds seven other spirits more evil than itself, and they all enter the person and live there. And so that person is worse off than before.*[42]

To be absolutely safe and secure from sin's power, one needs not only to be emptied of our selfish ways, but filled by the Spirit of God. To believe in Christ is to ask the one who died and rose from the dead to live within you. The Bible teaches: 'But to all who believed him and accepted him, he gave the right to become children of God.'[43]

Resist the devil

Having apologized for all that is wrong and believed in Christ, the Christian life is one of joyful union with God. This involves a daily renouncing of sin and resisting of Satan.

God promises that if we submit ourselves to Him we can 'Resist the devil and he will flee from [us]' and challenges us not to 'give a foothold to the devil'.[44]

Those who are prepared to take up the challenge to trust and live for the God who made them, died for them, and now calls, will be few. In the book of Revelation we read that the devil deceives the whole world and all those who live on earth.[45] Nevertheless, Jesus has promised His presence with those who do put their trust in Him: He has said to all His followers, 'I will never fail you. I will never abandon you.'[46]

A Royal Marine commando professed Christian conversion through the work of a missionary in the Royal Sailors' Rest in Singapore. Sadly though, he made no effort to change his lifestyle, and showed no signs of spiritual progress. He inevitably went back to living without any thoughts of God. Eventually his ship was to sail on, so the sailor went to the Christian worker to bid him farewell. The missionary said, 'I feel sorry for you.' Amused, the sailor retorted, 'Why?' The Christian took the sailor by the nose and pulled his head first in one direction and then another. 'I'll tell you why,' said the Christian. 'The devil has got you by the nose and is dragging you in any direction he wishes. And the trouble is, you love it.'

The Bible describes people being taken captive by the devil, at his will.[47] We need to realise that wrongdoing is attractive, especially in its early stages. The challenge is ours: will we follow Jesus or the devil? Do we belong to the kingdom of God or of Satan? Nobody can sit on the fence. There is no 'demilitarized zone' in the issues concerning God.

NOTES

1. John 14:30; 16:33
2. Colossians 2:15
3. James 4:7; 2 Corinthians 10:3–5; Ephesians 6:10–18
4. 1 Samuel 28:8
5. 1 Samuel 28:15
6. Isaiah 8:19
7. Peter Anderson, *Talk About the Devil* (Carlisle: Authentic, 1973)
8. Richard Wurmbrand, *Marx, Prophet of Darkness: Communism's Hidden Forces Revealed* (London: Marshall Pickering, 1986)

9. 1 Timothy 4:2
10. 1 Corinthians 10:10; John 8:44; Revelation 12:9; John 8:44; Ephesians 2:2; Genesis 3:1
11. 1 Peter 5:8
12. 2 Corinthians 4:4
13. John 10:10
14. 1 Thessalonians 2:18, NKJV
15. Matthew 12:39; 16:3–4; 24:24; Mark 8:12; 13:22; Luke 11:29,30; John 4:48
16. Isaiah 14:12–15
17. Job 1:9–11
18. 2 Peter 2:4
19. Revelation 13:8
20. Exodus 1:16
21. Esther 3:8–11
22. Matthew 2:16–18
23. Luke 4:28–30
24. John 8:58–59
25. Mark 4:35–41
26. Matthew 4:1–11; Luke 4:1–13
27. John 6:70–71
28. Matthew 27:42
29. 1 John 3:8
30. Hebrews 2:14
31. Warren Wiersbe, *The Bible Exposition Commentary*, Vol. 2 (Wheaton, ILL: Victor Books, 1989), p.506
32. John 16:8–11
33. Romans 3:23
34. John 3:16–18, 5:24, NKJV
35. Matthew 17:22–23; see also 20:18–19
36. Matthew 20:28
37. John 16:13–14

38. John 3:3
39. 2 Corinthians 5:17
40. John 8:32; Romans 6:23; John 8:12
41. Acts 19:19
42. Luke 11:24–26
43. John 1:12
44. James 4:7; Ephesians 4:27
45. Revelation 12:9; 13:14
46. Hebrews 13:5
47. 2 Timothy 2:26

3.

Why I Believe the World is Alienated from God

… all creation was subjected to God's curse. But with eager hope, the creation looks forward to the day when it will join God's children in glorious freedom from death and decay.[1]

When Sir Winston Churchill wrote his autobiographical volume, *My Early Life*, he was able to divulge intriguing details about himself. When he penned his *History of the English-Speaking Peoples*, by very definition it would have to remain incomplete. He could review the past and describe the present, but only God has a total view of the world and its unfolding drama. Past, present and future are all one in the eyes of a never-changing, timeless God.

His estimate of the world is comprehensive, fair and reliable. In contrast, ours is narrow, prejudiced and often misjudged. God sees tomorrow as He knows yesterday and today. So what is His view of the place that is our temporary home? How does God see the world? In the Bible, what do we read of planet Earth? We discover that:

The world was made by God

The opening sentence of the Bible is 'In the beginning God created the heavens and the earth.'[2] In the Bible, the Psalms say, 'The earth is the Lord's, and everything in it. The world and all its people belong to him. For he laid the earth's foundation on the seas and built it on the ocean depths.'[3] God created the earth and is owner of all His creation. Just as footprints convinced Robinson Crusoe of the existence of another human being on his island, so too there are imprints of the one who creates all over His creation – God is seen everywhere in the world.

An idealist in the French Revolution arrogantly said to a believer, 'We intend to tear down every memory of the idea of God.' Quietly, the Christian replied, 'How will you get down the stars?'

The work of creation is awesome; therefore it is realistic to believe that God created it. Behind every design is a designer; behind things made is a maker; behind creation is a Creator. Many dismiss Christianity and creation in the same way that one child looked up at a giraffe. It was the first time he had visited a zoo, and as he gazed at the long-legged, long-necked animal, he exclaimed, 'Ah, there's no such creature!' He had met something beyond his comprehension and outside his experience, so he concluded it could not be true. In contrast, read the words of King David in Psalm 8, written as he mused upon the wonder of creation.

> O Lord, our Lord, your majestic name fills the earth!
> Your glory is higher than the heavens …
> When I look at the night sky and see the work of your fingers –
> the moon and the stars you set in place –
> what are mere mortals that you should think about them,
> human beings that you should care for them?
> Yet you made them only a little lower than God

and crowned them with glory and honour.
You gave them charge of everything you made,
putting all things under their authority –
the flocks and the herds
and all the wild animals,
the birds in the sky, the fish in the sea,
and everything that swims the ocean currents.
O LORD, our Lord, your majestic name fills the earth!

The world has been ruined by sin

The world which was created without flaw or fault was beautiful and perfect, but experienced a moment of time when goodness and godliness were lost. There was an act of deliberate rebellion, when instead of becoming like God as had been promised to them by the serpent, Adam and Eve became like devils. The floodgate was opened. In rushed suffering, sickness and death like an uncontrollable torrent, so that the world has never been the same since. As the Bible puts it, 'Adam's one sin brings condemnation for everyone'; 'the world would never know him [God] through human wisdom'.[4]

Of course, God, who is infinitely understanding and compassionate, has heard the cries both of the cynics and of the suffering: 'If there is a God why doesn't He stop the trouble?' or 'Why does He appear to hide Himself in times of suffering?'

Psalm 10 describes corrupt people. They have three basic mistaken views of God. They argue that He does not exist (v. 4) and so is false; then they say He does not see (v. 11) or has forgotten their wrongdoing; and finally, they believe that He does not judge (v. 13), but offers blanket forgiveness. People are often ready to admit that they are not as good as they ought to be, yet at the same time feel they do not deserve God's judgement.

On 7 December 1985, Police Constable William Clements

gathered together his family for their daily Bible reading and prayer. Strangely, that day he read from Psalm 10, including the words found in verses 4–10:

> *The wicked are too proud to seek God.*
> *They seem to think that God is dead.*
> *Yet they succeed in everything they do ...*
> *Their mouths are full of cursing, lies, and threats.*
> *Trouble and evil are on the tips of their tongues.*
> *They lurk in ambush in the villages,*
> *waiting to murder innocent people.*
> *They are always searching for helpless victims.*
> *Like lions crouched in hiding,*
> *they wait to pounce on the helpless.*
> *Like hunters they capture the helpless*
> *and drag them away in nets.*
> *Their helpless victims are crushed;*
> *they fall beneath the strength of the wicked.*

In the afternoon he met another constable, and together they went to the police station in Ballygawley, County Tyrone, Northern Ireland, where they were based, to start their shift. Crouching in 'lurking places' of the village were terrorist gunmen who shot William Clements and his colleague dead, and then blew up the police station. He was a victim of the type of person described in the psalm. Jesus Himself fell prey to those who felt that God would not see their depraved deeds.

Verse 14 of the psalm reassures its readers that God not only exists, but that He does see and He will judge. However, at this present time, we live in a world that, although made by God, is marred by humankind. Because of our wrong, we have become enemies of the Holy God.

The form of sin may change, but the fact of it does not. Humanism has sought to call sin sickness, and excuse it, blaming wrongdoing on education, environment or ecology, but God's absolute standard and basis of morality remain the same. The psychologist Karl Menninger rightly asks through the title of his book, *Whatever Happened to Sin?*

God has given His unchanging law and uses it to make us aware of our true state. Two hundred words, engraved by the finger of God in tablets of stone, would condemn us all.

In Exodus 20 we read the Ten Commandments:

> *Then God gave the people all these instructions: ...*
> *You must not have any other god but me.*
> *You must not make for yourself an idol of any kind or an image of anything in the heavens or on the earth or in the sea. You must not bow down to them or worship them ...*
> *You must not misuse the name of the LORD your God ...*
> *Remember to observe the Sabbath day by keeping it holy.*
> *Honour your father and mother. Then you will live a long, full life in the land the LORD your God is giving you.*
> *You must not murder.*
> *You must not commit adultery.*
> *You must not steal.*
> *You must not testify falsely against your neighbour.*
> *You must not covet ...*

In attitude and action we all fall short. Covering up with respectability, religion or self-righteousness does not change our true nature. 'Wash a pig as much as you like, but it goes right back to the mud' says the Russian proverb.

Over and again, the Bible describes the world as failing. In Galatians we read of this 'evil world in which we live'; in

Ephesians of 'mighty powers in this dark world'; in Corinthians it speaks of 'Satan, who is the god of this world, [and who] has blinded the minds of those who don't believe. They are unable to see the glorious light of the Good News. They don't understand this message about the glory of Christ, who is the exact likeness of God.'[5]

No wonder one writer has described this world's system as 'rearranging the deck-chairs on the *Titanic* while it is sinking'.

As such, the picture painted is dark and dreary, but God has master-strokes that transform this whole view of the world.

The world has been reclaimed by Jesus

When speaking to individuals I often say, 'Jesus came into the world to save sinners … and you and I qualify.' Rarely does anyone disagree with that. Instead of God, godliness and goodness, the world's trinity is pleasure, treasure and leisure.

Despite the mad race for these, rarely is the world content. It appears orphaned. William Haddad was an associate of the Kennedys. After J.F. Kennedy was assassinated, his young son, John, asked Mr Haddad, 'Are you a daddy?' Haddad admitted that he was. Young John responded, 'Then will you throw me up in the air?'[6]

Similarly, the world searches for a fullness and fulfilment it cannot find because the vital link we were made to have between God and ourselves has been severed by sin. 'It's your sins that have cut you off from God. Because of your sins, he has turned away'.[7]

Into this type of world, Jesus was born. He came to take away the sin of us all. He is called 'the Saviour of the world'.[8]

After living a life that was pure and holy, He engaged in mortal conflict with the world, sin, the devil, death and hell. In the hours of darkness hanging on the cross He, like the world when it rebelled against God, was stripped of His dignity and covered with sin. All that keeps a person from God and would condemn

Him was laid on Jesus as He paid the price for the world's sin. God devised a means whereby we who are far from Him may be brought to Him through the death of his Son.

The significance of the cross is that God was in Christ reconciling the world to Himself. By raising Him from the dead, God demonstrated to a watching and waiting world Christ's triumph over sin.

The world will ultimately be restored and remade by God. God's plan for His creation is by no means over.

There have been many false prophecies. In 1901, Wilbur Wright predicted that there would be no powered flight for seventy years. Two years later, he was flying the skies. In the early 1970s, Margaret Thatcher said, 'There will not be a female prime minister in my lifetime'!

God, however, never makes false prophecies. He has a timetable for this world.

A little girl, returning home from school, stopped to listen to the market square clock chiming out the time. Something had evidently gone wrong, for it went on striking twelve, thirteen, fourteen, fifteen … She ran to her mother shouting, 'Mummy, it's later than it's ever been before!' As the King James Bible has it in Psalm 8:2: 'Out of the mouth of babes and sucklings'!

One day the world as we know it will cease. The apostle Peter wrote:

> *Then the heavens will pass away with a terrible noise, and the very elements themselves will disappear in fire … But we are looking forward to the new heavens and new earth he has promised, a world filled with God's righteousness.*[9]

In this time, Christ will be acknowledged as the King. This will be the world's greatest reclamation scheme. The history of the world will have gone full circle. It was made by God, ruined by sin, reclaimed by Christ, but will be restored and remade by God.

Interestingly, the history of the world is likewise the history of every true Christian.

Christians recognize that they are individually made by God

No birth is an 'accident'. God is in control, even though circumstances may sometimes be sad. Each person has been wonderfully made, and God has a perfect plan for everyone. To perceive this immediately brings a sense of responsibility. Watch a commercial van driver tearing round corners, screeching to a halt and burning up the tyres as he sets off at the lights. He treats the vehicle badly because he does not own it. If, however, he buys even a second-hand car for himself, how carefully that prized possession is cleaned, polished, driven and serviced. A sense of owning or being owned affects our behaviour. The point is not so much a political one as a theological one.

Atheists do not feel accountable to anyone, and declare themselves free of responsibility, but believers are aware that there is someone whose watchful eye weighs all actions and activities.

Christians are keenly aware that they have been ruined by sin

In the New Testament book of Romans, the apostle Paul lists Old Testament quotations to illustrate the sinfulness of each person.

No one is righteous – not even one.
No one is truly wise; no one is seeking God.
All have turned away; all have become useless.
No one does good, not a single one.
Their talk is foul, like the stench from an open grave.

Their tongues are filled with lies.
Snake venom drips from their lips.
Their mouths are full of cursing and bitterness.
They rush to commit murder.
Destruction and misery always follow them.
They don't know where to find peace.
They have no fear of God at all.[10]

Professor Hallesby, in his book *Religious or Christian?* says:

> *Men fill the world with their sins. Sins of every kind and of every degree: conscious sin and unconscious sin; individual sin and social sin; national sin and international sin; open sin and secret sin; sin that is afraid and conceals itself in dark places, and bold sin, openly committed. But the worst thing about man is not that he does that which is sinful. The unregenerate heart of man is worse that all his sinful deeds. For from within, out of the heart of men, proceed evil thoughts, adulteries, fornications, murders, thefts, covetousness, wickedness, deceit, licentiousness, an evil eye, blasphemy, pride, foolishness.*[11]

Christian hymn-writers have also expressed their consciousness of wrongdoing. For example, in his famous hymn *Rock of Ages*, Augustus Toplady wrote:

> *Nothing in my hand I bring;*
> *Simply to the cross I cling;*
> *Naked, come to Thee for dress;*
> *Helpless look to Thee for grace;*
> *Foul, I to the fountain fly;*
> *Wash me, Saviour, or I die.*

So many feel that their good works will hopefully give them a way to heaven, but everyone is guilty of sin. And sin, if not confessed to God and thereby forgiven and blotted out, is serious enough to keep us from the absolutely holy God forever. On almost the last page of the Bible, referring to heaven, it reads, 'Nothing evil will be allowed to enter, nor anyone who practices shameful idolatry and dishonesty'.[12]

In Mark 3, we read that Jesus met a man with a withered hand. Both were in the synagogue, where religious people would be looking on. Jesus commanded, 'Stretch out your hand.' Which hand was He speaking about? The answer appears obvious, namely the withered arm. Indeed, that is the one that was outstretched and healed by the power of Jesus. Most people, however, like to 'stretch out their good arm'. They speak of giving to charity, paying 100 pence in the pound, of never doing anybody any harm, or of attending church. Jesus cannot help such people because they are not wanting *Him*. He said that He 'came to seek and save those who are lost'.[13] If we would 'stretch out our withered arm' and confess our sins to God, we would find that 'he is faithful and just to forgive us our sins and to cleanse us from all wickedness'.[14] A sick person, not someone who is well, goes to a doctor. Similarly, only those who recognize their need will feel they must 'go to' Jesus Christ. A respectable Yorkshire parish church caused a stir when outside they hung a huge banner saying 'Only sinners welcome here'. They were right. That included everyone.

The Christian has been reclaimed by Jesus

True Christian experience begins when one enters into a living and personal relationship with God. Jesus died to buy us and to save us. Christians no longer belong to themselves. They have been bought through Christ's death and therefore belong to Him.[15]

Becoming a Christian is an act of God in the life of the person who, by an act of their mind and will, turn from their own ways to serve the living and true God.[16] At that moment God turns to the individual to forgive the past and guide the future. God can do this on the basis of the finished work of Jesus Christ.

The Bible teaches that God restores and remakes those who believe in Jesus

Jesus spoke of being 'born again' or 'born from above'.[17] Paul wrote, 'This means that anyone who belongs to Christ has become a new person. The old life is gone; a new life has begun!'[18]

In the moment of becoming a Christian, God by His Holy Spirit makes the new believer His dwelling place. As the years of Christian life begin to unfold, God refines the individual. Bad people are made good. Tempers are calmed, tongues are controlled, dishonesty and immorality are defeated, to be replaced with integrity and virtue. Ultimately, on that final, resurrection day, the work of sin will be totally reversed.

NOTES

1. Romans 8:20–21
2. Genesis 1:1, NIV
3. Psalm 24:1–2
4. Romans 5:18; 1 Corinthians 1:21
5. Galatians 1:4; Ephesians 6:12; 2 Corinthians 4:4
6. Clifton Fadiman (ed.), *Faber Book of Anecdotes* (London: Faber & Faber, 1985)
7. Isaiah 59:2
8. John 4:42; 1 John 4:14
9. 2 Peter 3:10,13

10. Romans 3:10–18
11. Professor Hallesby, *Religious or Christian?* (London: Inter-Varsity Fellowship, 1955)
12. Revelation 21:27
13. Luke 19:10
14. 1 John 1:9
15. 1 Peter 1:18–19; 1 Corinthians 6:19–20
16. 1 Thessalonians 1:9
17. See John 3:3,7
18. 2 Corinthians 5:17. See also chapter 5 of this book

4.

Why I Believe Jesus is the Son of God

Peter said: 'You are the Messiah, the Son of the living God.'[1]

Jesus said: 'The Father and I are one.'[2]

The most influential man of all time was born and reared in obscurity. He has changed the lives of millions. He has turned upside down the culture of nations. He has altered the course of world history.

Jesus Christ is the theme of the world's bestselling book, the Bible. Millions of other books and songs have been written about Him. So, who was Jesus of Nazareth? Christians believe He was absolutely human – He was 'God manifest in the flesh'.

Jesus Christ – a man
Jesus was conceived in the womb of a virgin. He was laid in a manger as a helpless baby. He grew to be a toddler, adolescent, young adult and mature man. He was subject to the authority of Mary and Joseph. As far as He was able, He conformed to the social and political conditions of the day.

Physically, Christ experienced hunger, thirst, weariness and pain, yet exercised self-control, self-denial, humility, calmness, endurance and wisdom.

Emotionally, Jesus was no stranger to joy and sorrow, wonder and amazement, love and anger, indignation and compassion. He used humour, yet wept at the tomb of His friend, Lazarus. He had an unswerving sense of duty and destiny.

Socially, Jesus was involved with the activities of people and society. He was invited to, and attended, the wedding feast at Cana in Galilee. He accepted invitations to meals. We read of His involvement in adult years with His mother, brothers and sisters. He had special friends and valued companionship. Even in His last moments on the cross, Christ made provision for His mother and beloved disciple, John, giving each responsibility for the other. Jesus was distant and yet accessible.

Jesus was not the 'hippy' drop-out philosopher He is sometimes portrayed as being. His thinking and teaching were intuitive, spiritual and practical. He was not an echo of other voices, but the original voice. His teaching was not abstract or negative, but concrete and positive.

No wonder that twenty centuries on from the completion of His life on earth, there is profound interest and fascination in His life and work. Even the greatest sceptics prove by continually speaking of Him that He is a man they cannot leave alone.

Jesus Christ – a mighty man

On examination of the gospels of Matthew, Mark, Luke and John, Christ is seen clearly portrayed as being more than 'head and shoulders' above others.

Jesus never apologized, nor needed to. He did not blush with embarrassment or shame. He never had to withdraw a word. He showed no sign of regret or remorse. Jesus did not suffer the pain of an accusing conscience. In fact, He was bold enough to ask His enemies, 'Which of you can truthfully accuse me of sin?'[3] That is not a question most of us would dare throw about. Such was the character and calibre of the life of Christ that even men like Judas, who betrayed Christ for a mere thirty pieces of silver, later committed suicide having cried, 'I have sinned ... for I have betrayed an innocent man.'[4] Pilate, who sentenced Jesus to crucifixion, appealed to Christ's accusers asking, 'Why? What crime has he committed? I have found no reason to sentence him to death.'[5] The Roman executioner said of Him, 'This man truly was the Son of God!'[6]

The goodness of Jesus is demonstrated in His attitude to people. He loved His enemies; He was patient with His friends; He met the needs of the crowds; He went alongside outcasts; He delighted to do the will of His Father in heaven; and He died willingly, paying for our sin.

There were no character defects in Christ. He was not only without sin, but without weakness also. There was an equilibrium and balance of personality in Christ. He demonstrated great haste and energy, but He also knew how to rest and be still. He could be very severe, but deeply tender and compassionate. He was a man of great dignity and stature, but humbled Himself to wash the feet of His disciples (including Judas), and eventually even to death on the cross. While needing times of solitude, He was sociable; solemn, but joyful, and greatly profound, but attractively straightforward.

Jesus Christ – more than a man

To be true to the Bible's teaching about Jesus Christ is to accept that our minds and intellect are unable to understand all things. Some things are beyond human comprehension. No one can ever fully fathom the God who has revealed Himself as infinite, inexhaustible and eternal.

However, the Bible clearly teaches that God became a man. God clothed Himself in a human body. God was big enough to become small, strong enough to become weak – as small and weak as a tiny foetus in a mother's womb, later to be a little baby wrapped in swaddling clothes and laid in a manger. This was the great Maker of all becoming like the people He had made – the Creator becoming as one of His creatures.

In a school nativity play, a little boy appeared as the third wise man. However, when he came on stage he saw his mother and father sitting in the audience and was utterly awestruck. His lines went as his mind went completely blank. Eventually, he knelt down to present the myrrh to 'baby Jesus'. He just could not remember what to say. After an embarrassing silence, the exasperated teacher whispered, 'Say something!' Instead, silence still reigned. 'Say anything,' called the teacher in desperation. Suddenly the boy blurted out, 'Eh, He's just like His Dad!'

The Creator did come to earth, and He was 'just like' His Father. He was destined by God to go to the cross, to save this world. Rising again, He was to ascend to heaven.

Colonel James Irwin of the Apollo XV Mission was right when he said, 'God walking on earth is more important than man walking on the moon.'

There are many reasons to believe that Jesus is God incarnate. Here are four:

He is called what only God is called
Both the Old and New Testaments speak of Jesus being God. Repeatedly in the Old Testament, the Messiah's coming and work is prophesied. Around 700 BC, Isaiah says: 'For a child is born to us, a son is given to us. The government will rest on his shoulders. And he will be called: Wonderful Counsellor, Mighty God, Everlasting Father, Prince of Peace.'[7]

Micah, writing about 710 BC, said: 'But you, O Bethlehem Ephrathah, are only a small village among all the people of Judah. Yet a ruler of Israel will come from you, one whose origins are from the distant past.'[8]

In the Old Testament, there are over seven thousand references to the sacred name of God, usually written as Yahweh or Jehovah, but originally given to Moses as 'I AM'. In Exodus 3:14, in response to Moses' question to God as to what he should call God, we read, 'God replied to Moses, "I AM WHO I AM." Say this to the people of Israel: "I AM has sent me to you."' In the New Testament, God's name is written as 'Lord'. This exalted title is applied directly to Jesus.[9] Clearly Jesus is Jehovah. In fact, Jesus took God's own title to refer to Himself, calling Himself the 'I AM'.[10] Muslims like to say that Jesus never said He was God. That argument is based on not realizing that Jesus did not speak English! Time and again, Jesus used the language of His day taking the name of God used at that time and applying it to Himself. Repeatedly, Jesus called Himself the 'I AM'. That led some to accuse Him of blasphemy, claiming to be God.

Over forty times, New Testament writers call Jesus the 'Son of God'. This name is associated with Him in His baptism, in His temptations, His miracles and His sufferings.[11]

Five times Jesus is called 'the only begotten Son of God'.[12] The word 'begotten' is an important one: 'It indicates that, as the Son of God, he was the sole representative of the being and character of the one who sent Him.'[13]

Jesus is called 'the Alpha and Omega … the First and the Last'.[14] Repeatedly, the New Testament clearly calls Jesus God. For example, we read:

> *In the beginning the Word already existed. The Word was with God, and the Word was God ... So the Word became human and made his home among us.*[15]

> *No one has ever seen God. But the unique One, who is himself God, is near to the Father's heart. He has revealed God to us.*[16]

Meeting the risen Jesus, whom Thomas had doubted, we read his words, *'My Lord and my God!'*[17]

Speaking of the church, the apostle Paul describes it as *'God's flock – his church, purchased with his own blood'.*[18]

> *But to the Son he says, 'Your throne, O God, endures forever and ever.'*[19]

> *Christ ... is God, the one who rules over everything and is worthy of eternal praise!*[20]

> *Look! The virgin will conceive a child! She will give birth to a son, and they will call him Immanuel, which means 'God is with us.'*[21]

> *We look forward with hope to that wonderful day when the glory of our great God and Saviour, Jesus Christ, will be revealed.*[22]

Even Jesus' preferred self-designation 'Son of Man' carries great significance. The title comes from the Old Testament where the Son of Man, who is a heavenly figure, appears at the close of history as the judge, lord and heir of all the kingdoms of the world.[23] It is a title particularly bound up with the idea of judgement, which is a role reserved exclusively for God.

Very plainly, Jesus is called what only God is called.

He is like what only God is like

Too often people create their own image of God. One hears statements such as, 'My view of God is … ' Frankly, an individual caricature of God is of little importance. What is vital is God's revelation of His own character. That is exactly what the Bible is – the revelation of God.

It describes four basic attributes of God: His omnipotence (total power), His omniscience (total knowledge), His omnipresence (total presence), and His immutability (total changelessness). We also read that He is alive forever, sinless, just, loving, holy and consistent.

The Bible reveals God as a Trinity. He is one God in three distinguishable persons. Human thought and language are strained to try and grasp or explain this infinite truth. God would not be God and humans would not be human if we could fully comprehend Him. Each person of the Trinity is divine: the Father is God; the Son is God; and the Holy Spirit is God.[24] As one Christian hymn expresses it:

Holy, holy, holy! Merciful and mighty!
God in three persons, blessed Trinity![25]

Jesus' godliness can be seen in that His attributes are uniquely God's. Yet since He was God confined by the human body in which He was 'dressed', there were clearly self-imposed limitations on these attributes.

Although choosing to lay aside His omnipotence, Jesus nevertheless repeatedly demonstrated His power. On one occasion, He was asleep in the stern of a boat on the Sea of Galilee. A severe storm suddenly blew; the disciples, in a state of panic, awakened Him, crying, 'Teacher, don't you care that we're going to drown?' Jesus immediately stilled the storm with the words, 'Silence! Be still!' The wind ceased and there was a great calm. Understandably the disciples said one to another, 'Who is this man? Even the wind and waves obey him!'[26] With this same power, Christ fed over five thousand with just five loaves and two fishes. He cured the lame and leprous, the blind, deaf and mute and the paralysed. He cast out demons and even raised the dead. Then, after the resurrection, God gave to Jesus all authority, and raised Him up, seating Him at His right hand.[27] He is truly all-powerful.

In Luke's gospel, we see Jesus learning and listening.[28] We read of Him at the age of 12 sitting in the midst of the doctors of the law talking and asking questions. However, even at such a young age He left these learned men astonished at His understanding and answers. We then read that He continued to increase in wisdom and stature. It was the same Jesus who was later to show that He knew the secret whisperings of both the disciples and those who plotted against Him, by revealing their thoughts. Today He is the one from whom nothing is hidden; He knows the details of all our lives. Jesus is all-knowing.

Then, we see God who is present everywhere, confined to human form in Jesus Christ. During His earthly ministry, Christ was in only one place at a time. However, looking forward to a time after His resurrection, Jesus made promises such as: 'For where two or three gather together as my followers, I am there among them.'[29] And 'I am with you always, even to the end of the age.'[30] These assurances are grounded on Jesus' omnipresence.

As far as Jesus' unchanging nature is concerned, we read in the Bible:

> *[Jesus] existed before anything else, and he holds all creation together.*

But you [Jesus] are always the same; you will live forever.

Jesus Christ is the same yesterday, today, and forever.[31]

As Jesus revealed His absolute God-like attributes to His disciples, so they realised their own sinfulness. When Peter saw Christ's omniscience, He cried, 'Oh, Lord, please leave me – I'm too much of a sinner to be around you.'[32]

What it must have been for the disciples to spend their years with Christ, who is described as 'holy', 'blameless', 'unstained by sin' and 'set apart from sinners'.[33] They bickered and quarrelled, He did not. They showed pride and selfishness, He would not. They sinned, He could not.

John, who was especially close to Jesus, said, 'In him is no sin'; Paul, the great thinker, said, 'He knew no sin'; Peter, the man of action, said, 'He did no sin'; and the book of Hebrews sums it up with the categorical 'He is without sin'. Only God is so pure.

We see Jesus demonstrating God's love and justice throughout His life in all His dealings with people. Different needs were met. His love was never at the expense of justice, nor was His justice devoid of love. Love and justice met at the cross. Apparently opposing forces met together perfectly when Jesus died. It was infinite love for rebellious creatures, such as we all are, that took Jesus to His death. Neither Roman soldiers nor nails held Jesus to the cross, but love. The arms of Christ were outstretched as if to go to every nook and cranny of every human heart to draw to Himself the wrong of us all. God's justice judged the sin of all by instead punishing Jesus the substitute, so as to be able to forgive us, the sinners. 'Christ suffered for our sins once for all time. He never sinned, but he died for sinners to bring you safely home to God.'[34]

He acts as only God acts

God is an active God. Activity and work are intrinsically bound up in the nature of God (and incidentally, in those who would follow Him).

The work of Jesus was such that it can only be explained as being of God. This is seen in four ways.

His creation

In every great act of God, the Trinity is at work. We read in Genesis that God said, 'Let us make human beings in our image, to be like us.'[35] The plurality of the persons of God is seen here in the use of the words 'us' and 'our'. God spoke, the Spirit hovered over the face of the waters, but 'God created everything through him [Jesus], and nothing was created except through him'[36]

Later, in the Bible, the apostle Paul wrote:

> *Christ is the visible image of the invisible God. He existed before anything was created and is supreme over all creation, for through him God created everything in the heavenly realms and on earth. He made the things we can see and the things we can't see – such as thrones, kingdoms, rulers, and authorities in the unseen world. Everything was created through him and for him.*[37]

If God is the Creator, and the Creator is Christ, then Christ is God!

His teaching

People say, 'Practice what you preach'; Jesus preached what He practiced. His life and teachings were utterly consistent. His words were original, straightforward, profound, picturesque, concrete, practical, brief and authoritative. He rarely quoted others, but no one has been so often quoted. He never wrote a book, but libraries are 'full of' writing concerning Him. He spoke, and others silently listened. Nothing He said has had to be corrected with the passing of time, but the world is still to see one person who will fully obey His teaching. Religious officers who were sent by the Pharisees and chief priests to trap Him, came back and reported, 'No man ever spoke like this man.'[38] They were more right than they imagined. No wonder we read that the common people heard Him gladly.

His miracles

The miracles of Christ can only be explained by the power of God at work. C.S. Lewis has argued:

> *The miracles ... are a retelling in small letters of the very same story which is written across the whole world in letters too large for some of us to see ... In other words, some of the miracles do locally what God has already done universally: others do locally what He has not yet done, but will do.*[39]

For example, when Jesus turned water into wine at Cana in Galilee, He was taking off the mask. Each year God turns water into wine. He creates the vine so that it draws up water by its roots and, with the sun's help, turns that water into a juice that will ferment and take on certain qualities. We call it a law of nature. Jesus' miracle was simply shortcutting the process.

Or again, year-by-year God turns a little corn into much corn – the seed is sown and there is an increase. Similarly, in every lake and river the slow process of the multiplication of fish is constantly at work. However, when Jesus fed both the 5,000 and the 4,000 He short-circuited this process. A little bread and a few fish were miraculously multiplied to feed the crowds. Christ's work was God's work with the mask off.

The miracles of healing fall into the same pattern. The work of healing is not so much in the medicine but the patient's body (it would be no use bandaging a dead body; there must be life for there to be recovery). Jesus cured people visibly and instantly, again cutting short the inward process with which we are more familiar.

Jesus only does what He sees the Father do.[40] As C.S. Lewis puts it, 'There is, so to speak, a family style.'[41] Christ's miraculous work is evidence of His being God: He was doing the work of God.

His death

Death and mortality have no part in the existence and being of God, who is eternal. Death came into this world as a result of sin. God had warned Adam, 'You may freely eat the fruit of every tree in the garden – except the tree of the knowledge of good and evil. If you eat its fruit, you are sure to die.'[42] Jesus never sinned and therefore death could not touch Him. He could say to a group who were His enemies, 'No one can take my life from me. I sacrifice it voluntarily. For I have the authority to lay it down when I want to and also to take it up again.'[43]

Yet strangely, Jesus was the only person born to die. In fact, He was the only one who chose to die (in contrast to a person who commits suicide, who merely decides when he dies, not whether he dies). However, when Jesus was crucified He was fulfilling God's plan to save men and women, the Old Testament pictures and prophecies, as well as His own aim and purpose.

Jesus was not just a martyr or example. His death was not merely a quirk of history, but rather a central part of God's greatest act. Hanging on the cross in agony, humiliation and shame, God transferred the sin of the world on to Him.

God took the sins of wrong attitudes and actions; sins of the past, present and future; the sins we have forgotten and those we wish we could forget; the wrong we regret and that in which we revel; then laid them all upon Christ. The sins of millions were put on Him. Such a crushing load contracted and compacted into three hours would have killed any other instantly. However, Jesus – God in human form – carried them all.

To carry such a load, to be able to pay the eternal punishment in three hours of terrible suffering, is sufficient evidence that Jesus is Himself God. 'God was in Christ, reconciling the world to himself'.[44]

His resurrection

Throughout the ages, the names of conquerors have come and gone – Alexander, Julius Caesar, Napoleon, Hitler. One conqueror has, however, defeated them all. That is the conqueror 'death'. Herod killed the baby boys in Bethlehem, Nero the Christians in Rome, Hitler the Jews and a host of others, and Stalin his political opponents; but the conqueror 'death' has been totally indiscriminate – except for one.

Jesus died, was buried and rose from the dead. No other religious founder or leader has ever done that.

The historical evidence for this great event is absolutely watertight. Jesus Himself had prophesied it. For example, He said, '"Destroy this temple, and in three days I will raise it up." ... But when Jesus said "this temple", he meant his own body.'[45] The disciples and others were witnesses to it. Jesus' opponents could not explain it and hundreds of early Christians experienced it.

This is not a cunningly devised fable, nor Christian mythology, but an historical event. Examining the evidence, we see that:

(a) There is no doubt that He was dead

Before the crucifixion, the back of Jesus had been beaten with many lashes. They had buffeted Him, spat on Him and wedged a crown of thorns on His head. He was made to carry on His torn back a rough, rugged Roman cross. Nailed through His hands and feet, He was suspended up on the wooden beams. He drank nothing to alleviate the pain. Over and above the physical and emotional hurt was the spiritual suffering. Jesus, the innocent one, took the sin of the world on Himself. After doing so, He triumphantly cried out, 'It is finished!' and voluntarily 'released his spirit' as John's gospel records.[46]

Professional executioners, as the Roman guards were, saw that He was dead, but just to ensure it, they thrust a spear into His side. Blood and water poured out, showing that there had been certain death.[47]

(b) There was no opportunity for the body to be stolen

Jesus' corpse was laid in the tomb in the evening before sunset. Cloth was wrapped around His body and head separately.[48]

A huge stone was rolled in front of the tomb and a guard placed around it to prevent His body from being stolen. The soldiers themselves would be under threat of death if the body disappeared. On the third day, which became the first Easter Sunday morning, the stone had been rolled away to reveal that though the clothing was left intact, the body of Jesus had gone – He had risen from the dead.

(c) There is no possibility of it being a lie

During the next forty days, Jesus appeared to various groups of people including two women, two men walking to Emmaus, first of all two, then ten, and then the eleven disciples, as well as to a group of over five hundred at one time.[49]

These resurrection appearances were such that the antagonistic authorities were unable to dispute them. They were in different circumstances at different times and in varying places. Neither the Romans nor the Jews, who would have loved to have disproved the resurrection of Jesus by producing His corpse, were able to refute the facts: the tomb was empty, with the body not only gone, but the living Jesus appearing to many people. Most of the disciples were to die for their testimony, that they had seen the risen Christ alive. Would they do this for a lie?

(d) There is no explanation except that Christ rose from the dead
It was a clear resurrection from the dead – not mystical or spiritual, but physical. To the disciples, Jesus said: 'Look at my hands. Look at my feet. You can see that it's really me. Touch me and make sure that I am not a ghost, because ghosts don't have bodies, as you see that I do.'[50]

Thomas's reaction to the risen Christ is the only sufficiently expressive one. He simply exclaimed, 'My Lord and my God!'[51]

In the forty days after the resurrection, Christ appeared many times. He completed His teaching to the disciples and brought them to a confident assurance of His defeat of death.

It was a final, climactic appearance that brought Jesus' work to a completion. This happened when a cloud manifesting God's presence and glory took Him away. This, plus His present exaltation and His promised return,[52] are confirmation of the person of Jesus as Lord, God and Saviour.

He claims what only God claims
If you were God, how would you get the attention of the world – by a lightning bolt or a message in the sky?

So often God's method has been to send a baby. When He was to deliver the people of Israel from Egypt, God sent the baby Moses; when He was to judge Israel righteously He sent a baby – Samuel; when He was to prepare the way for the coming of Christ, God sent the baby John; and when the one who would save the world was to come, He came in the form of a baby.

Whereas others have pointed the way to God, Jesus pointed to Himself as the way: 'Jesus called out to them, "Come, follow me, and I will show you how to fish for people!"' or, 'Come to me, all of you who are weary and carry heavy burdens, and I will give you rest.'[53] This was not arrogance or megalomania. He is the unique way to God. He said, 'I am the way, the truth, and the life. No one can come to the Father except through me.'[54] If Jesus was not God, this would have been delusional vanity, but millions have proved the truth of His claims.

He claimed to give life, something only God can give. He said, 'I give them eternal life, and they will never perish. No one can snatch them away from me'.[55] Jesus promised a truly satisfying life: 'But those who drink the water I give will never be thirsty again. It becomes a fresh, bubbling spring within them, giving them eternal life.'[56] And God, in offering this life, is not a disappointment.

Jesus claimed to be able to forgive sin. On one occasion, Jesus said to a paralysed man, 'My child, your sins are forgiven.'[57] Some scribes immediately questioned this statement, saying that He was speaking in the place of God, because only He can forgive sins.

Jesus is God, and because of His death and resurrection offers to all who will trust Him new life. This is an offer only God can make.

Jesus, the God-man, deserves to be the God of your life.

NOTES

1. Matthew 16:16
2. John 10:30
3. John 8:46
4. Matthew 27:4
5. Luke 23:22
6. Matthew 27:54
7. Isaiah 9:6
8. Micah 5:2

9. 1 Peter 3:22 applies Psalm 110:1; Romans 10:13 applies Joel 2:32; Philippians 2:9–11 applies Isaiah 45:23; see also John 12:41 and Ephesians 4:8 which applies Psalm 68:18

10. Exodus 3:14; cf. John 8:58; 6:35; 8:12,24; 10:7,11; 11:25;14:6; 15:1; 18:5ff.; Mark 14:62

11. Mark 1:11; Matthew 4:3,6; Matthew 16:16, Mark 15:39

12. Most modern translations of the Bible, though, translate 'begotten' as 'one and only' reflecting the fact that the word has passed from everyday usage

13. W.E.Vine, *New Testament Word Pictures: Romans to Revelation* (Nashville: Thomas Nelson: 2015), p.1092

14. Revelation 1:8,17; 22:13

15. John 1:1,14

16. John 1:18

17. John 20:28

18. Acts 20:28

19. Hebrews 1:8

20. Romans 9:5

21. Matthew 1:23

22. Titus 2:13

23. Daniel 7:13

24. Matthew 6:8ff.; 7:21; Galatians 1:1; John 1:1,14,18; Romans 9:5; Colossians 2:9; Titus 2:13; Hebrews 1:8–10; Mark 3:29; John 15:26; 1 Corinthians 6:19; 2 Corinthians 3:17ff.

25. 'Holy, Holy, Holy! Lord God Almighty', Reginald Heber, 1783–1826

26. Mark 4:35–41

27. See Matthew 28:18; Ephesians 1:19–23; Philippians 2:8–11

28. Luke 2:41–52

29. Matthew 18:20

30. Matthew 28:20

31. Colossians 1:17; Hebrews 1:12; Hebrews 13:8

32. Luke 5:8

33. Hebrews 7:26

34. 1 Peter 3:18

35. Genesis 1:26

36. John 1:3

37. Colossians 1:15–16

38. John 7:46

39. C.S. Lewis, *God in the Dock* (Fount Paperbacks, 1979)

40. John 5:19

41. C.S. Lewis, *God in the Dock*

42. Genesis 2:16,17

43. John 10:18

44. 2 Corinthians 5:19

45. John 2:19–21

46. John 19:30

47. John 19:34

48. John 20:5–7

49. Many are mentioned in 1 Corinthians 15

50. Luke 24:39

51. John 20:28

52. Acts 1:9–11

53. Matthew 4:19; 11:28

54. John 14:6

55. John 10:28

56. John 4:14

57. Mark 2:2–12

5.

Why I Believe Death has been
Defeated by God

*... that through death He might destroy him who had
the power of death, that is, the devil, and release those
who through fear of death were all their lifetime subject
to bondage.*[1]

Woody Allen famously said that he was not afraid to die, but he
didn't want to be there when it happened. His quote vocalizes the
silent fears of most people.

Ironically, we give our lives to learning to live, but before the
lessons are fully learnt, life is taken from us.

Life is so short. The Bible likens it to a tale that is told; to a
vapour, which is here one minute and gone the next; to a shadow;
to the speed of a weaver's shuttle in a loom; to grass or flowers
blooming for a few days but then being cut down and withering.
There is a mark on many tombstones that is highly significant.
Between the dates of birth and death is a hyphen. It is just a small
dash. Such is life: a short span between birth and death.

Inevitably, there is grieving at the loss of a member of a family,
when a friend, colleague or neighbour is taken by death. Death is
separation. Physical death is the severing of the link between the

human spirit and body. 'For then the dust will return to the earth, and the spirit will return to God who gave it'[2] is how the Bible describes death.

Death can take many forms. In moral death, a person's life becomes devoid of, or separate from, all moral convictions. When a person dies intellectually, they close down their minds from all new ideas and intellectual pursuit. Some die socially, isolating themselves from the fabric and friendship of society. Spiritual death is the result of sin, and afflicts every human being until the human spirit is born again. Sin separates us from our Creator.

Fear of death holds captive each person, who will eventually and inevitably become its victim. Yet, the Christian gospel offers an answer to death. It has been conquered. This is nowhere better expressed, than in Paul's letter to the Christians living in Corinth: 'For sin is the sting that results in death, and the law gives sin its power. But thank God! He gives us victory over sin and death through our Lord Jesus Christ.'[3]

Looking at the teaching of this biblical statement and seeing its most salient points, notice first:

The grave

The grave is inevitable. The verse talks about 'the sting that results in death'. Nobody knows when they will die, though they know they must. I have only met one person so utterly deceived that she really felt she would never die. The awful reality for her error will one day dawn on her. Obviously, we cannot go through life constantly thinking of the day of death, but we need to be sure that we are at least ready for it. I could not enjoy the journey if I felt that the end was to be a crash landing!

For eight years, I worked with a Christian man who died of cancer, aged 47. Though a tireless lay preacher, his most powerful sermon was preached in his last five or six weeks, after he had

been told that he only had days in which to live. He had such
confidence of his home in heaven, which Christ had made possible
for him. A friend telephoned to ask him of his health, and as it was
explained the caller remarked, 'So it's only a matter of time?' 'Yes,'
replied the patient, 'but it is for you too, isn't it?'

All of humanity is travelling along a path that leads each
individually through the turnstile of death.

Frequently the Bible reminds us of the inevitability of death.
King David said, 'But I swear to you that I am only a step away
from death! I swear it by the LORD and by your own soul!'[4]
Understanding what God's Word has to say about death prepares
us for the time we will be taken in its clutches.

A widow who lived in Tekoa wisely said, 'All of us must die
eventually. Our lives are like water spilled out on the ground, which
cannot be gathered up again.'[5] In the Bible, the book of Job describes
its namesake's suffering and the reality of death which had been
vividly brought home to him through the loss of his children. His
groaning can be heard between the lines of much that he spoke.[6]
In the Psalms we read, 'But you will die like mere mortals and fall
like every other ruler.'[7] The 'weeping prophet' Jeremiah cried out,
'For death has crept in through our windows and has entered our
mansions. It has killed off the flower of our youth'.[8]

In the New Testament we read, 'And … each person is destined
to die once and after that comes judgment'.[9] The apostle Paul
wrote to Timothy saying, 'After all, we brought nothing with us
when we came into the world, and we can't take anything with us
when we leave it.'[10]

God and we know the date of our birth. Only God knows the
date of our death. We have to admit, with the patriarch Isaac, 'I
don't know when I may die.'[11]

There is an old legend about a merchant in Baghdad who one
day sent his servant to the market. Before very long, the servant

came back, pale and trembling and in great agitation said to his master: 'Down in the marketplace I was jostled by a woman in the crowd, and when I turned round I saw it was Death that jostled me. She looked at me and made a threatening gesture. Master, please lend me your horse for I must hasten away to avoid her. I will ride to Samara and there I will hide and Death will not find me.'

The merchant leant him his horse and the servant galloped away in great haste.

Later the merchant went down to the marketplace and saw Death standing in the crowd. He went over to her and he asked, 'Why did you frighten my servant this morning? Why did you make that threatening gesture?'

Death responded, 'It was not a threatening gesture, it was only a start of surprise. I was astonished to see him in Baghdad for I have an appointment with him tonight in Samara.'

The nineteenth-century evangelist D.L. Moody never forgot the childhood memory of hearing the bells of his village church in New England tolling out at funerals the age of the person who was to be buried. It was not always the old; often there were just a few chimes.

While the Stalins and Hitlers of this world murdered their targeted opponents by the millions, death makes no such discrimination. Death gives no reprieve, but keeps all it has taken. Young and old, rich and poor, good and bad, famous and insignificant are captured by this last enemy.

The gift

Secondly, after the diagnosis comes the remedy. After the grave, the verse tells us of the gift: 'But thank God! He gives us victory'.

The testimony of countless Christians is one of quiet confidence of God's presence in them in life, through death, and on into eternity. This is not based upon a vain superstition.

Instead, relying on the finished work of Christ, that He died and rose, the Christian has claimed forgiveness of sin that Jesus died to offer, as well as His constant and everlasting companionship.

For the Christian, though death may destroy the body, it cannot touch the soul or spirit. At the moment of becoming a Christian, an everlasting link is established between God and the individual. As Paul wrote: 'And I am convinced that nothing can ever separate us from God's love. Neither death nor life, neither angels nor demons, neither our fears for today nor our worries about tomorrow – not even the powers of hell can separate us from God's love.'[12]

'We all have thoughts that would shame even hell,' wrote Robert Louis Stevenson. Call it hypocrisy, selfishness, failure or weakness, it is nevertheless sin that is the sting of death. Would there be death at all if there had been no sin? Would anyone fear death if we could pass through it with a clear conscience? Surely not! The unknown future may appear daunting, but it is made dreadful because of the known past.

If there is certainty that when death comes we will live on with God in eternity, then there need be no fear of leaving and laying aside the body.

Patricia St John wrote Christian stories for children. She expresses this truth so well in her book *The Tanglewoods' Secret*. Terry, a Christian gypsy boy, has died. His friend Ruth is grieving alone when she meets a wise old yokel called Mr Tandy, whom she questions.

'They buried Terry in the earth and we left him there, and it seemed so sad and lonely. How can Terry be with the Shepherd when we left him lying in the earth?'

The old man did not answer for a moment, and then he started scraping about with his hands in the leaf-fall as though he were looking for something. His search was rewarded and he held out a shiny brown conker in one hand, and an empty seed box in the other – a withered old thing with green prickles turning brown.

'Now tell me,' he said, in his, slow, thoughtful voice, 'what's a-goin' to happen to the conker, and what's a-goin' to happen to the covering?'

'Oh,' I answered, 'the case will get buried in the leaves and then I suppose it will just wither away. It isn't needed any more; but the conker will grow roots and leaves and turn into a chestnut tree.'

'That's right,' said Mr Tandy, encouragingly. 'Ye couldn't have said it better; now, tell me this, little maid; when you see the young chestnut tree a-waving its little new leaves in the sunshine next spring, with the birds a-singing round it, and the rain a-watering of it, you ain't goin' to fret any more for that old case what's crumbled under the leaves, be you?'

'No-o,' I answered, with my eyes fixed on his face. Once more I thought I understood.

'Well, then,' said the old man, triumphantly, 'you cease fretting for what you laid below ground – t'weren't nothing but the case. The laddie's a-growing strong in the sunshine up yonder, along of his Saviour.'

His kind old eyes lit up with joy as he spoke; he threw down the conker and case, shouldered his axe and rose stiffly to his feet, because his knees were 'full of rheumatics' as he had once told me. Then be bade me go home.[13]

Jesus' disciple Peter, knowing he was soon to die and leave his body, wrote, 'For our Lord Jesus Christ has shown me that I must soon leave this earthly life' but had written about a 'place reserved in heaven' for all those who have put their trust in Jesus.[14]

The same certainty has been experienced by Christians countless times.

Susannah Bicks was a sweet Christian girl. In 1664, aged 14, she was about to die in Holland. Her last words were, 'Father, you see that my body is this tabernacle which shall be broken down; my soul shall now depart from it, and shall be taken up to heaven.'

John Newton, converted slave trader and author of the hymn *Amazing Grace*, quaintly said before his death in 1807, 'I am like a person going on a journey in a stage-coach, who expects its arrival every hour, and is frequently looking out of the window for it ... I am packed and sealed, and ready for the post.'

Henry Martyn, missionary to India and Iran and Bible translator, a day or two before his death in 1812 wrote in his diary:

> *I sat in the orchard and thought with sweet comfort and peace, of my God in solitude – my Companion, my Friend, and Comforter! O, when shall time give place to Eternity? When shall appear that new heaven and new earth wherein dwelleth righteousness? There shall in no wise enter in anything that defileth; none of that wickedness that has made men worse than wild beasts –none of those corruptions that add still more to the miseries of mortality shall be seen or heard any more.*

In May 1987, the USS *Stark* was missiled by an Iraqi jet fighter. Thirty-seven American marines died. The front page of *The New York Times* on 21 May printed a photograph of five-year-old John Kiser, the son of one of the dead sailors. He was standing with his hand on his heart, watching the coffin of his father as it was unloaded at Washington airport.

Mrs Kiser was interviewed by the press. *The New York Times* reported that she said she didn't have to mourn or wear black for she knew her husband was in heaven, and she was happy because she knew he was better off.

Later the US Ambassador in Bahrain said that Mrs Kiser and her son had given him a letter and a New Testament, translated into Arabic, to be sent to the pilot of the Iraqi plane. He would deliver the package, addressed to 'The men who attacked the *Stark*, Dad's ship', to the Iraqi Ambassador in Bahrain, 'in the hope that he will send it to the pilot to show that even the son ... and the wife do not hold any grudge and are at the same time praying for the one who took the life of the father.'

Rev. Mark Ashton, vicar of St Andrew the Great Church in Cambridge, and greatly loved by students in the city, died of cancer in 2010. His final words were, 'Soon home!'

The Giver

Thirdly, in this text we see the one who gives. He, of course, as we see in the verse, is Jesus Christ. His gift is of infinite value, for He paid an infinite price to be able to offer it to us all. The cost was not the sacrifice of perishable things such as silver or gold, but His own precious blood.[15]

The gift, which in this verse is victory in the face of death, also includes as part of the package forgiveness, new spiritual life, God's power to live day by day, His total presence through all situations, as well as a host of other blessings in which Christians delight. The gift is not to be worked for or earned, for it would cease to be a gift. If we receive our due payment, we would be lost forever. Heaven is not a reward; it is a gift. The Bible says, 'For the wages of sin is death, but the free gift of God is eternal life through Christ Jesus our Lord.'[16]

When Jesus healed the sick, raised the dead or taught the crowds, He did not ask for payment or contribution. People did not have to work to earn His favour. The gospel is always freely given. Christ the giver paid the infinite price, for God was in Christ reconciling the world to Himself.

Sin is so serious that it must be punished infinitely and eternally. Either the sinner, who is finite, must be infinitely punished, or the infinite substitute (Jesus) must suffer for a finite length of time. Jesus was God manifest as a man. In the dark hours on the cross, without sin ever contaminating Him, Jesus became sin for us and carried the guilt that would condemn us eternally.

Jesus died so that we might live. He suffered so that we might enjoy His peace. He rose from the dead, defeating death and the grave.

A family was enjoying a peaceful picnic when suddenly their little girl began to panic and scream. A bee was flying near to her face. Nothing consoled her until the father stood up and swiped the bee. As he did, it stuck to him and stung him, shook itself and flew away. The father then turned to his daughter and said, 'You're all right now. A bee can only sting once and I have taken the sting in your place.'

Jesus did the same. He took the sting of death. He was stung by our sin so that we might be saved from it. He can release us from the power of sin, death and hell to give us life forever. He has tasted the bitterness of death for everyone. He died to atone for sins which were not His own, but ours.[17] A Christian is a person who has received the gift of forgiveness from God, the giver.

The gratitude
This is the fourth idea found in the verse. We read, 'But thank God … ' Jesus, having loved us and given Himself for us, demonstrates such a great and undeserved expression of love that the recipient becomes overwhelmed and overflowing with thankfulness. The Apostle Paul was so deeply grateful that he said of Christians that

they are not their own, but have been bought with a price. He felt that with just food and clothing he was content because Jesus Christ meant so much to him.

Only the Christian can say over the open grave 'Thanks' or 'Victory'. This is not to minimize death. It is still an enemy. Christians grieve. Jesus wept at the tomb of His friend, Lazarus, even though He knew that He would raise him back to life. But Christians do not sorrow as others who have no hope.[18]

I remember reading to a dying friend the poem, 'Cancer is so limited'. Then, seconds before he was in eternity, my wife whispered in his ear, 'John, you will very soon be in the presence of the Lord Jesus. He is altogether lovely.'

Cancer is so limited …
It cannot cripple love,
It cannot shatter hope,
It cannot corrode faith,
It cannot eat away peace,
It cannot destroy confidence,
It cannot kill friendship,
It cannot shut out memories,
It cannot silence courage,
It cannot invade the soul,
It cannot reduce eternal life,
It cannot quench the Spirit,
It cannot lessen the power of the resurrection,
Cancer is so limited.

Have you trusted Jesus as your Lord and Saviour? Have you given your life to Him, as your natural response to His deserved rights over you? A life lived for self and sin is an expression of ingratitude for His love.

To be, as the Bible expresses it, absent from this body is to be present with the Lord.[19] Jesus said to the dying thief who was crucified next to Him and who repented and believed, 'I assure you, today you will be with me in paradise.'[20]

How different will be the destiny of those who refuse Christ and His gift!

A Salvation Army woman went up to a prostitute standing on the streets in Soho, who was quite abusive to the Salvationist. The woman persisted until she was told to 'Get lost'. Lovingly, as she turned away, the woman said, 'My dear, you are lost.' The prostitute never forgot those haunting words that were so descriptive of her life.

Where will you spend eternity?

Jesus, who loved so much, wooed people to heaven and warned them of hell. The Bible says, 'The wicked will go down to the grave. This is the fate of all the nations who ignore God.'[21] Jesus Himself spoke of it as a place of 'weeping and gnashing of teeth.'[22] He spoke of those on His left hand being told, 'Away with you, you cursed ones, into the eternal fire prepared for the devil and his demons.'[23] Perhaps most poignant of all is the story told by Jesus in Luke 16. The sugar-sweet Christianity that is prevalent in the West today has often overlooked this striking passage, but reading it carefully makes the reality of eternity abundantly clear.

Jesus told of a rich man whose rejection of God was shown by his neglect of his neighbour, a poor beggar. One lived on earth in great comfort, the other in such desperation that he longed for the crumbs that fell from the rich man's table. However, in eternity, the rich man was in hell but the beggar, whose name, Lazarus, means 'in God I trust', was with God. In the passage there are no actions such as murder, adultery or robbery. But to leave out God from a life is the greatest of all sins.[24] As C.S. Lewis expressed it, 'The safest road to hell is the gradual one – the gentle slope, soft underfoot, without sudden turnings, without milestones, without signposts.[25]

Occasionally, the awful horror of humanity's inhumanity or sinfulness pierces our hearts and emotions. Something within us cries out for justice, sometimes for vengeance. But vengeance belongs to God. The Bible says that He will repay.[26] The sins to which we have grown accustomed, be they wrong thoughts, words, actions, or lack of right actions, God has consistently hated. He has always demanded that such wrongdoing be punished.

The revelation of God, the Bible, and the resurrection of Jesus both show that there is life after death. The Bible makes plain that God will one day judge each individual.[27] There are some who say that everybody will eventually be saved, but the same Greek word in the Bible that speaks of eternal separation from God is used to describe the eternity of heaven.[28] After death there is no second chance. The Bible nowhere teaches purgatory. God's judgement will usher in an everlasting, conscious existence either in heaven or in hell. C.S. Lewis said, 'Once a man is united to God, how could he not live for ever? Once a man is separated from God, what can he do but wither and die?'[29]

There are many passages in the Bible that teach that there is hell for those who willingly and knowingly reject Christ as Saviour:

> *He will come with his mighty angels, in flaming fire, bringing judgment on those who don't know God and on those who refuse to obey the Good News of our Lord Jesus. They will be punished with eternal destruction, forever separated from the Lord and from his glorious power.*[30]

> *'I am in anguish in these flames.'*[31]

> *But cowards, unbelievers, the corrupt, murderers, the immoral, those who practice witchcraft, idol worshipers, and all liars – their fate is in the fiery lake of burning sulphur. This is the second death.*[32]

Can a loving God send a person to hell? The answer is that He can, but always reluctantly. People who refuse to turn from wrong to receive God's mercy and forgiveness condemn themselves. Like a sick patient refusing the doctor's remedy, so many stubbornly resist God's love towards them. God, who is both just and loving, must punish sin. A better question is, how can a just God *not* send people to hell? And the answer is bound up in all that Jesus accomplished on the cross.

The resurrection of Jesus is God's receipt that Christ's payment for sin on the cross has been accepted. Heaven is promised to all who put their trust in the Lord Jesus:

> *All praise to God, the Father of our Lord Jesus Christ. It is by his great mercy that we have been born again, because God raised Jesus Christ from the dead. Now we live with great expectation, and we have a priceless inheritance - an inheritance that is kept in heaven for you, pure and undefiled, beyond the reach of change and decay. And through your faith, God is protecting you by his power until you receive this salvation, which is ready to be revealed on the last day for all to see.*[33]

The prophet Ezekiel who lived over five hundred years before Christ, had a vision that has been popularized by the Afro-American spiritual, *Dem Bones*. This is how he described it in chapter 37 of his book:

The LORD took hold of me, and I was carried away by the Spirit of the LORD to a valley filled with bones. He led me all around among the bones that covered the valley floor. They were scattered everywhere across the ground and were completely dried out. Then he asked me, 'Son of man, can these bones become living people again?'

'O Sovereign LORD,' I replied, 'you alone know the answer to that.'

Then he said to me, 'Speak a prophetic message to these bones and say, "Dry bones, listen to the word of the LORD! This is what the Sovereign LORD says: Look! I am going to put breath into you and make you live again! I will put flesh and muscles on you and cover you with skin. I will put breath into you, and you will come to life. Then you will know that I am the LORD."'

So I spoke this message, just as he told me. Suddenly as I spoke, there was a rattling noise all across the valley. The bones of each body came together and attached themselves as complete skeletons. Then as I watched, muscles and flesh formed over the bones. Then skin formed to cover their bodies, but they still had no breath in them.

Then he said to me, 'Speak a prophetic message to the winds, son of man. Speak a prophetic message and say, "This is what the Sovereign LORD says: Come, O breath, from the four winds! Breathe into these dead bodies so they may live again."'

So I spoke the message as he commanded me, and breath came into their bodies. They all came to life and stood up on their feet – a great army.[34]

He went on to explain that the symbolism pictured the nation of Israel at that time. In God's economic use of words, however, they seem to depict another truth, which is applicable to all.[35]

At the end of time as we know it, there is to be a resurrection of the dead, when spirit and soul, whether with God or lost from Him, will be joined again to a resurrection body.

This is not fairy-tale speculation, but a theme running through the Bible. See, for example, in Job: 'And after my body has decayed, yet in my body I will see God!'[36]

In Isaiah we read: 'But those who die in the LORD will live; their bodies will rise again! Those who sleep in the earth will rise up and sing for joy! For your life-giving light will fall like dew on your people in the place of the dead!'[37]

The book of Daniel says: 'Many of those whose bodies lie dead and buried will rise up, some to everlasting life and some to shame and everlasting disgrace.'[38]

In Matthew's gospel we read that Jesus said: 'And he will send out his angels with the mighty blast of a trumpet, and they will gather his chosen ones from all over the world –from the farthest ends of the earth and heaven.'[39]

In John's gospel, Jesus says: 'But anyone who eats my flesh and drinks my blood has eternal life, and I will raise that person at the last day.'[40]

Paul said, in the book of Acts: 'I have the same hope in God that these men have, that he will raise both the righteous and the unrighteous.'[41]

In 1 Corinthians we read: 'It is the same way with the resurrection of the dead. Our earthly bodies are planted in the ground when we die, but they will be raised to live forever.'[42]

Philippians says: 'I want to know Christ and experience the mighty power that raised him from the dead. I want to suffer with him, sharing in his death … '[43]

The last Bible book, Revelation, describes how 'The sea gave up its dead, and death and the grave gave up their dead. And all were judged according to their deeds.'[44]

There is coming a moment when 'grave-breaking' will begin.

Many, long since dead, will hear the voice of God, and perhaps those who have never heard the voice of God before will be 'awakened' on this great day.

As two types of people have lived and died, so two types will rise. People who trusted Jesus and knew God, and those who rejected Him; those whose trust has been placed in Jesus, and many who relied on themselves; those destined for heaven and those destined for hell.

Everyone will rise: the octogenarian and the infant; kings and politicians; both good and bad; great men and beggars; armies of victors and vanquished; men and women murdered by weapons, in fires, by guillotines, or who rotted in dungeons; the shipwrecked and the lone victim of the heat of a desert; people buried in great pomp and ceremony, and those who were never buried. Millions from the continents and countries of the world will rise at the command of the all-powerful, all-knowing God.

As crystals dissolve in liquid only to reappear when heated to evaporation point, so the dust of the earth, which once absorbed the body of the deceased, will, on the appointed day, give up its dead.

In eternity, the Christian's resurrection body will be glorious, immortal and powerful. There will be no wrinkles, stoops, grey hairs, deformity, ailments, disease, groans, nor coughs. There will be work without weariness, no night, and no need for sleep.

The wrong of the person who neglects or rejects God will appear so great then because it will be seen in the true light.

It is not only some modern-day sceptics who find it hard to comprehend all this teaching. Twenty centuries ago, Paul met the same questioning. He answered authoritatively and concluded triumphantly. Read what he wrote to Christians long ago:

But someone may ask, 'How will the dead be raised? What kind of bodies will they have?' … What I am saying, dear brothers and sisters, is that our physical bodies cannot inherit the Kingdom of God. These dying bodies cannot inherit what will last forever.

But let me reveal to you a wonderful secret. We will not all die, but we will all be transformed! It will happen in a moment, in the blink of an eye, when the last trumpet is blown. For when the trumpet sounds, those who have died will be raised to live forever. And we who are living will also be transformed. For our dying bodies must be transformed into bodies that will never die; our mortal bodies must be transformed into immortal bodies. Then, when our dying bodies have been transformed into bodies that will never die, this Scripture will be fulfilled:

> *'Death is swallowed up in victory.*
> *O death, where is your victory?*
> *O death, where is your sting?'*

For sin is the sting that results in death, and the law gives sin its power. But thank God! He gives us victory over sin and death through our Lord Jesus Christ.

So, my dear brothers and sisters, be strong and immovable. Always work enthusiastically for the Lord, for you know that nothing you do for the Lord is ever useless.[45]

Do you know the Christ who has defeated death and who is willing to live within you?

NOTES

1. Hebrews 2:14–15, NKJV
2. Ecclesiastes 12:7
3. 1 Corinthians 15:56–57
4. 1 Samuel 20:3
5. 2 Samuel 14:14
6. Job 7:1–3, for example
7. Psalm 82:7
8. Jeremiah 9:21
9. Hebrews 9:27
10. 1 Timothy 6:7
11. Genesis 27:2
12. Romans 8:38–39
13. Patricia St John, *The Tanglewoods' Secret* (Milton Keynes: Scripture Union, 1948), p.146. Used by permission; all rights reserved
14. 2 Peter 1:14; 1 Peter 1:4, NKJV
15. 1 Peter 1:18–19
16. Romans 6:23
17. See Hebrews 2:9–18; John 8:51–52
18. 1 Thessalonians 4:13
19. 2 Corinthians 5:8
20. Luke 23:43
21. Psalm 9:17
22. Matthew 22:13
23. Matthew 25:41
24. Luke 16:19–31
25. C.S. Lewis, *The Screwtape Letters* (Fount Paperbacks, 1982)
26. Romans 12:19
27. 2 Corinthians 5:10; Hebrews 9:27; Revelation 20:11–15
28. Matthew 25:46

29. C.S. Lewis *Mere Christianity* (1952; Harper Collins: 2001) pp.176-177
30. 2 Thessalonians 1:7–9
31. Luke 16:24
32. Revelation 21:8
33. 1 Peter 1:3–5
34. Ezekiel 37:1–10
35. See Galatians 4:24: 'These ... serve as an illustration.'
36. Job 19:26
37. Isaiah 26:19
38. Daniel 12:2
39. Matthew 24:31
40. John 6:54
41. Acts 24:15
42. 1 Corinthians 15:42
43. Philippians 3:10
44. Revelation 20:13
45. 1 Corinthians 15:35, 50–58

6.

Why I Believe Christians are Children of God

But to all who believed [Jesus] and accepted him, he gave the right to become children of God.[1]

There is a creative instinct in each person. After all, we were made in the image of God the Creator. So, if you were able to create a human being, what sort of being would you come up with?

No doubt, he or she would have a physical dimension. Each one produced would have a unique body with size and shape. The body is important, but not all-important. Every few weeks, I have part of mine amputated. But I don't weep as the barber sweeps up the cuttings. They are only a part of my body.

I heard a doctor explain that the body contains enough lime to whitewash a hen coop, enough iron to make a nail, enough phosphorous to tip 2,200 matches, enough sulphur to rid a dog of fleas, enough potash to blow up a toy car, enough sugar to sweeten six cups of tea, enough fat to make seven bars of soap – and the whole lot is worth only a few pounds sterling.

We all know that there is more to us than a mere conglomeration of atoms and cells covered with skin. The body is like a shell or casing, which houses the real person.

Would you also make human beings with intellectual ability? Surely our facility to reason and act reasonably is one of our greatest attributes. Four centuries ago, Galileo Galilei rightly said, 'I do not feel obliged to believe that the same God who has endowed us with sense, reason and intellect has intended us to forego their use!' We are able, with the use of our brain, to be analytical, intuitive, artistic and verbal.

What an awful individual, though, would be a human with great intelligence, yet who had no feelings, emotions or heart. A man or woman is more than a body-with-a-mind.

Would you also make humans social beings? One of the great joys of human existence is the ability to socialize. Interaction with the opposite sex and companions of the same sex may be delightful or at times disturbing, but it is part of our *raison d'être*. We are social beings and were formed for society. As God created the earth and everything in it at the beginning of time, He repeatedly said that 'it was good'.[2] The first time God said something was not good was when, having created Adam, he stated, 'It is not good for the man to be alone.'[3]

Is that all that there would be to the person you created? Would you not also want to impart something of your life into him or her? When God created people, He made them higher than any other form of life – vegetable or animal. Humans have a spiritual dimension to their existence. We read in Genesis, 'Then God said, "Let us make human beings in our image"'; 'Then the LORD God formed the man from the dust of the ground. He breathed the breath of life into the man's nostrils, and the man became a living person.'[4] Like animals, men and women are creatures of earth; unlike them, they can become citizens of heaven. People have the ability to know, appreciate, enjoy and worship God. The life of the living God can live in the life of a human being. The dust of men and women was created to be filled with the life of the Creator.

There was a time when God and humanity walked together in perfect harmony. There was a relationship unspoilt by the sin or selfishness of human beings. The spiritual life of God's new creation was alive and well. Man and woman were complete, enjoying their God, each other and the world around them.

But people were not created as puppets on strings or electronic robots. They were made with the challenge, freedom and responsibility of the ability to make choices. Instead of obeying God, they deliberately rebelled against Him. It was never God's desire for us to discover evil, whatever its source, but Adam and Eve took the fruit of the tree of the knowledge of good and evil.

Man and woman had been made so intricately in the image of God that the least flaw would transform them into the very image of the devil. As a result of their sin, paradise lost was now their domain. Their spiritual nature died, so that all born of man and woman since have been born spiritually dead. Immediately, we see Adam and Eve on the run from God, who Himself took the initiative in tenderly seeking them: 'Then the LORD God called to the man, "Where are you?"'[5]

How many millions have been born since? Different cultures and colours of skin, backgrounds and beliefs, personalities and parentage form the vast array of the teeming multitudes. All are alike in that their greatest need is to be reconciled to God so that they might be made spiritually alive. We were made with a physical, intellectual, social and spiritual dimension, but with that spiritual nature dead, we are incomplete.

Not all are as outwardly bad as others. Jesus Himself spoke of it being more tolerable on judgement day for some than for others, though all the groups of which He spoke were nevertheless lost from God.[6]

Philosophers and theologians have in times past argued that there are, as it were, different kinds of existence. These are nothing to do with class or status, but attitudes and actions. The lowest level of human existence (let us call it level one) is the type of person who is guided by nothing but their own desires. If these people have any urge, they follow their 'instinct' to fulfil these desires. Their motto is summarized by the common expression, 'If it feels good, do it.' They are guided by their impulses, passions and lusts. They will do anything to satisfy and gratify their physical desires or perverted minds. Though often described by onlookers as behaving like animals, that is far from the truth. Such people were made to know God, but sin has devastated their spiritual life, ruining every part of them. Spiritual death brings in its wake total death. Some in this category have become household names for their wickedness.

The Bible describes such people:

> *When you follow the desires of your sinful nature, the results are very clear: sexual immorality, impurity, lustful pleasures, idolatry, sorcery, hostility, quarrelling, jealousy, outbursts of anger, selfish ambition, dissension, division, envy, drunkenness, wild parties, and other sins like these. Let me tell you again, as I have before, that anyone living that sort of life will not inherit the Kingdom of God.*[7]

On a higher level (level two) is the vast majority of the population. These are the crowd followers. They are enslaved by soap operas on television, buy what is advertised because everybody else is buying it, and their conversation is inconsequential and trivial. Their views and politics are determined solely by what is expressed by their peers or in the media. They do not think individually and would never take a lone stand against current trends or their peer group. As the Bible says, they 'think up foolish ideas … their minds became dark and confused.'[8] They may be pleasant people trying to be kind and helpful, but they are not the people they were originally created to be.

Perhaps the third level is the group of people who are governed by reason. Their constant appeal is to common sense. They have a conscience and earnestly seek to follow it, even if it is a costly stand for them. These have been prominent in the news because they have often been 'thorns in the flesh' of corrupt or inept governments, totalitarian regimes or dictatorial tyrants. Their logic, knowledge, insight and courage may be admirable, but they still fall short of the glory for which we were created.

These three levels describe 'natural' people instead of 'spiritual' men and women. Some may even be religious, but they do not enjoy a personal relationship with the one who created them. They do not know God.

There is, however, a fourth level, whereby individuals are guided by the Spirit of the living God who lives in them. Such people have each come to a moment in their lives when they have asked Jesus Christ to rid them of past sin, and by His Holy Spirit to actually come as a welcome guest to dwell in their lives, to take control of them and bring them into an intimate relationship with God. He, through their mind and reason, guides them. They in turn daily seek to bring their life, feelings, actions and will under the control of God. They are experiencing what one writer called 'the life of God in the soul of man'.

Examples of becoming a child of God

Becoming a son or daughter of God is nothing to do with social class or background. They are not people who were born with a religious 'bent'! And the spiritual life is not something that is attained, earned or worked up to. It is received as a gift from God. There is not a slow evolution from level one to two to three to four, but rather a miracle from heaven itself in the life of men and women, whose only qualification is that they are sinners. 'This is a trustworthy saying, and everyone should accept it: "Christ Jesus came into the world to save sinners" – and I am the worst of them all' said the apostle Paul.[8] Jesus said, 'For I have come to call not those who think they are righteous, but those who know they are sinners.'[9]

John Newton had become a 'level one' individual. His life appeared to be one long drama. Son of an English sea captain, John went to sea at 11 years of age, and eventually became a slave-ship captain during the worst years in the traffic in slaves when inhuman treatment of black people was legal and normal. His language and life betrayed his savage mind. His own epitaph on his grave in Olney, Buckinghamshire, describes him as an infidel and libertine. Here is how he describes, in eighteenth-century English, what led to his conversion:

> I went to bed that night in my usual security and indifference, but was awakened from a sound sleep by the force of a violent sea, which broke on board us; so much of it came down below as filled the cabin I lay in with water. This alarm was followed by a cry from the deck, that the ship was going down or sinking ... Another person went up [and] was instantly washed overboard. We had no leisure to lament him, nor did we expect to survive him long; for we soon found the ship was filling with water very fast. The sea had torn away the upper timbers on one side, and made a mere wreck in a few minutes. Taking in all circumstances, it was astonishing, and almost miraculous, that any of us survived to relate the story ... We expended most of our clothes and bedding to stop the leaks ... I told one of [my companions], that in a few days, this distress would serve us to talk over a glass of wine; but he being a less hardened sinner than myself, replied, with tears, 'No; it is too late now.' About nine

o'clock … just as I was returning from seeing the captain, I said almost without any meaning, 'If this will not do, the Lord have mercy upon us.' This (though spoken with little reflection) was the first desire I had breathed for mercy for the space of many years. I was instantly struck with my own words; and, it directly occurred, 'What mercy can there be for me?' I was obliged to return to the pump, and there I continued till noon, almost every passing wave breaking over my head; but we made ourselves fast with ropes, that we might not be washed away. Indeed, I expected that every time the vessel descended in the sea, she would rise no more; and though I dreaded death now, and my heart foreboded the worst, if the Scriptures, which I had long since opposed, were indeed true; yet still I was but half convinced, and remained for a space of time in a sullen frame, a mixture of despair and impatience. I thought, if the Christian religion was true, I could not be forgiven.[10]

But forgiven he was. His cry for mercy was heard. The ship sailed on and he was saved. He had the desire to see his life transformed. He came into contact with Christians, and was eventually to leave sailing and the slave trade to become an Anglican clergyman.

This formerly savage man was the author of hymns such as *How Sweet the Name of Jesus Sounds* and *Amazing Grace*. He was taken from level one to level four in an instant of time. His cry for mercy was heard by the one who hears the faintest whisper of those who call out to Him. John Newton was sincere in his repentance and faith towards Christ, and found forgiveness, and was given spiritual life.

As far as level two is concerned, there are countless millions of people who, though unknown as far as the world is concerned, are known to God. John Newton lived 200 years ago. Alf and Sandra Tipper of Leigh in Lancashire found that Newton's God could become theirs. Alf, a laundry manager, told their story in the *United Beach Mission* magazine:

> *It was the first real holiday for my wife, Sandra, and our two children, Becky and Alex. It was also our first visit to picturesque St Ives in Cornwall, and the first time we ever saw a United Beach Mission Team ... The children enjoyed the games and competitions, and like all good holidays it seemed to be over all too soon. I vividly remember setting off on the long journey home with two happy little voices singing, 'He made the stars to shine' from the back seat of the car until they fell asleep.*
>
> *We enjoyed that holiday so much that we booked again at St Ives for the next two years in succession, and each time the United Beach Mission was there. We chatted to the team on the beach, and stopped to listen in the evenings as they held their open-air meetings at the harbour.*
>
> *Sandra has always believed in God, had gone regularly to church as a girl and had taught in Sunday school before getting married. She had always thought herself as much a Christian as anyone else. It was a shock to realise, as she listened to the message, that she was not a Christian at all! Despite her religious background she had never known God personally for herself, or given him any place in her life.*
>
> *One team member gave her a copy of John's Gospel and asked her to promise to read one chapter a day until she had read it all. In fact, that same night in our holiday flat she read it straight through, not putting it down until she had read every word. She told me later, 'There were tears in my eyes as I realised that Jesus had died on that cross for me. Jesus had taken my punishment, and now I had a chance to "start again". I saw myself as I really was – stubborn, selfish, and guilty before God. So in the privacy of that bedroom I prayed and asked God to take*

over my life and make me a better person. The next morning I woke up and realised that I now knew what being a Christian really meant – I had become one!'

When we returned home I soon noticed a change in Sandra – for one thing, she never seemed to stop talking about God and he seemed so real to her! She read her Bible, prayed, and wanted to go to church – things she was not doing before! I liked this 'new' Sandra, and we began to attend regularly as a family at a local Bible-believing church.

On the beach I had been cynical, dismissing the team as 'religious nuts'. On more than one occasion I had pretended to be asleep to avoid having to talk to them! But underneath it all, I knew that they were right. I had a foul mouth and a foul temper, and I was ashamed of my life when I compared it with theirs. I knew that unless I did something about it, I was lost. In the November of that year we were invited to a bonfire party at the home of some Christian friends we had met on the beach mission. They had a peace and contentment in their lives that really showed, and I knew it was lacking in mine. I wasn't singing with them, and I knew why – I wasn't part of them because I didn't know God for myself as they did. By the dying embers of that bonfire I silently asked God to become real to me too and change me. I believe he did answer that prayer, became ever since then I have been aware of him in a way I never knew before.

All this happened some years ago now. You might ask, has becoming a Christian worked? Has it lasted? As to how much God has changed our lives, others must be the judge. All we can say is that we still feel the same about him, and have never lost that sense of a personal, living relationship, and we still attend church as a family.

Ordinary people, on level two, met the extraordinary God and were taken to level four of humanity.

Why I Believe

A former professor of medieval and Renaissance literature at Cambridge University, and prolific author of books like the Narnia series and *Mere Christianity*, is my example of a level-three man. C.S. Lewis was for many years an atheist, but he relates, 'In the Trinity Term of 1929 I gave in, and admitted God was God ... perhaps the most dejected and reluctant convert in all England.'

In his autobiography, *Surprised by Joy*, he describes his feelings at the time of conversion:

> *The odd thing was that before God closed in on me, I was in fact offered what now appears a moment of wholly free choice. In a sense. I was going up Headington Hill on the top of a bus. Without words and (I think) almost without images, a fact about myself was somehow presented to me. I became aware that I was holding something at bay, or shutting something out. Or, if you like, that I was wearing some stiff clothing, like corselets, or even a suit of armour, as if I were a lobster. I felt myself being, there and then, given a free choice. I could open the door or keep it shut; I could unbuckle the armour or keep it on. Neither choice was presented as a duty; no threat or promise was attached to either, though I knew that to open the door or to take off the corselet meant the incalculable. The choice appeared to be momentous but it was also strangely unemotional. I was moved by no desires or fears. In a sense I was not moved by anything. I chose to open, to unbuckle, to loosen the rein. I say, 'I chose,' yet it did not really seem possible to do the opposite. On the other hand, I was aware of no motives. You could argue that I was not a free agent, but I am more inclined to think that this came nearer to being a perfectly free act than most that I have ever done. Necessity may not be the opposite of freedom, and perhaps a man is most free when, instead of producing motives, he could only say, 'I am what I do.' Then came the repercussion on the imaginative level. I felt as if I*

*were a man of snow at long last beginning to melt. The melting
was starting in my back – drip-drip and presently trickle-trickle.
I rather disliked the feeling.*[11]

Academic prowess was not sufficient to satisfy the God-shaped
gulf in the life of C.S. Lewis. Only God could fill that.

Has such a moment of becoming a Christian ever happened
to you? Has your sin been forgiven? Are you right with God? Do
you have spiritual life? Are you certain of heaven? Are you a child
of God?

The marks of a child of God

The apostle Paul had not yet visited the city of Rome, the capital
of the Roman Empire, when he wrote to the group of Christian
believers who were living there. He was concerned that they
should fully grasp the essence of Christian belief, so in his letter
to the Romans, in the New Testament, he straightforwardly
outlines the gospel message. In chapter 8, he lists some of the
characteristics of being a child of God.

A child of God belongs to God (v. 15)

They can actually talk to God as their Father. There is a family tie.
Nothing can separate a Christian from the love of God. After all,
Christ actually died out of love for people. If, then, a person receives
the gift of forgiveness, how warm will be the welcome, and how
real the relationship between God and the new family member.

A child of God will talk to God (v. 15)

He will pray. Prayer is not just an emergency rip-cord to pull in times
of great extremity; it is the means of speaking to God our Father.
Prayer is the lifeline between God and us. It is the spontaneous
consequence of a new bond established by Christ Himself.

If you never pray, ask yourself, 'Am I really a Christian?' God reassured the Christian leader, Ananias, that Saul of Tarsus had truly been transformed, with the words, 'He is praying to me right now.'[12] Even the weakest Christian will want to start to pray with a few words of thanksgiving, praise, confession of sin and requests to God.

A child of God knows their heavenly Father (v. 16)

The Christian relationship with God is not casual or platonic. There is a knowledge of God that goes so deep that it stimulates an ever-growing desire for more of God. Can a cross-Channel swimmer claim to know the English Channel? Maybe, but there is so much more than 23 miles in a more or less straight line. There is the vastness of the sea with which to become familiar. In like manner, though the Christian knows God, it will be a lifelong desire to know God more and more. He is not a dull personality with whom one quickly tires, but the infinite God whose loving person is such that He stirs within the Christian a heart that needs Him.

A child of God will want to walk with God (v. 14)

If He loved us enough not to spare His own Son, but freely delivered Him up for us, then we can implicitly trust Him. God guides those who are guidable. He has general desires for all and specific plans for each individual who trusts Him. As Christians, we will not want to rush ahead like a horse, or lag behind like a mule, but simply walk with God, at His pace and in His direction.

A child of God is called to suffer (v. 17)

Jesus said, 'If any of you wants to be my follower, you must turn from your selfish ways, take up your cross daily, and follow me.'[13] God said of Saul of Tarsus, who had just become a Christian, 'for Saul is my chosen instrument to take my message to the Gentiles and to kings, as well as to the people of Israel. And I will show him how much he must suffer for my name's sake.'[14] Paul himself wrote, 'everyone who wants to live a godly life in Christ Jesus will suffer persecution'.[15] A Christian is swimming against prevailing tides and trends. The world is at enmity with God and will be at enmity with those who are His friends and family. When all speak well of us, we will need to examine very carefully our relationship with God. When God is the one we seek to please, those who keep God out of their thinking will not be pleased.

A child of God is an heir (v. 17)
Finally, God is the Father of all who truly believe. All that is His is ours. Jesus promised that the meek shall inherit the earth.[16] Through Jesus' work on the cross, and the Holy Spirit's work in us, God has made Christian people His own for ever. In fact, the Holy Spirit guarantees our inheritance.[17] What an inheritance He is. There are many exceedingly great and precious promises throughout the Bible in which God assures His people that He works all things together for good, overruling evil and undertaking for His sons and daughters.

Becoming a child of God
How then can a person become a part of God's family? We are not children of God by birth. We are all created by Him, but need to be brought into His family.

Jesus talked about 'being born again', or being 'born from above.'[18] This involves a completely new start. It is a change in nature that God brings about in the heart of an individual. The Bible also speaks of adoption:

But when the right time came, God sent his Son, born of a woman, subject to the law. God sent him to buy freedom for us who were slaves to the law, so that he could adopt us as his very own children. And because we are his children, God has sent the Spirit of his Son into our hearts, prompting us to call out, 'Abba, Father.'[19]

The word 'adoption' is used because it teaches that we once belonged to someone other than God, but now there has been a change in our position before God. We have a standing before Him as sons and daughters, if we have trusted Christ.

The phrase 'born again' has caught the imagination of people in recent years. Advertisers, politicians and preachers have used the term. It originated when, under the cover of darkness, a religious leader approached Jesus with a statement that would have flattered or fooled a lesser man. 'Rabbi,' said Nicodemus to Christ, 'we know that You are a teacher come from God; for no one can do these signs that You do unless God is with him.'

Jesus simply replied, 'Most assuredly, I say to you, unless one is born again, he cannot see the kingdom of God.'[20]

Understandably, Nicodemus, despite the fact that he had great theological training and was renowned for his ability in things religious, was bewildered. In the quietness of the night, he took his opportunity to question Jesus further. There was no attempt to proudly cover up his ignorance, rather an honest seeking, as Nicodemus continued:

'How can an old man go back into his mother's womb and be born again?' Jesus replied, 'I assure you, no one can enter the Kingdom of God without being born of water and the Spirit. Humans can reproduce only human life, but the Holy Spirit gives birth to spiritual life. So don't be surprised when I say, "You must

be born again." The wind blows wherever it wants. Just as you
can hear the wind but can't tell where it comes from or where it is
going, so you can't explain how people are born of the Spirit.'[21]

The nineteenth-century preacher Henry Drummond had a helpful illustration of what it means to be born again. He said that there are many levels of 'kingdoms' in this world: from the lowest, the mineral kingdom, to the vegetable kingdom, the animal kingdom, the human kingdom and the highest, God's kingdom. He then argued that it is a basic law of the universe that no kingdom can lift itself up to a higher level. For example, a stone cannot become a rose. A rose, likewise, cannot become a rabbit. A rabbit cannot become a human, and no human can become God. However, it is also a basic law of the universe that each kingdom can reach down and pull a lower one up. For example, the vegetable kingdom can reach down into the mineral kingdom and turn it into grass. From the animal kingdom, a cow can chew the grass and turn it into flesh. Then the butcher turns the cow's flesh into steak, which is eaten by a human, so that what is animal becomes human.

God through Christ has come to this world and can reach down to lift us up. Now humans can be 'born from above' or 'born again'. All of us have been born of water. That was our physical birth. But there needs to be a new birth, which is the start of spiritual life.

Note first that Jesus said, 'You *must* be born again' (my italics). Nicodemus was deeply religious, strictly following disciplines of prayer, devoutly seeking to keep religious law, yet still he had to be born again. Indeed, no matter how hard any of us may try to understand spiritual things, we simply cannot receive them until we have been born again by the Holy Spirit. Paul explains this in his first letter to the Corinthian Christians.[22] There is no spiritual life until the new birth: there is no everlasting life unless there is a new birth. New birth is the only passport to heaven. How many times I have asked people if they are certain of heaven, only to be told, 'I hope so! I've never done anybody any harm.' I always feel, 'Who is fooling whom?' We all do harm. We are all guilty of doing wrong, which keeps us from God and would condemn us. The only hope lies in the fact that Jesus taught that there is a new birth.

Has this ever happened to you? Have you been born again?

Secondly, you *may* be born again. Jesus said, 'And the judgment is based on this fact: God's light came into the world, but people loved the darkness more than the light, for their actions were evil.'[23] Those who are lost from God are guilty of deliberately resisting all the obstacles that God would put in the path of those heading away from Christ.

Be careful – the day you stopped attending Sunday school, refused to pray, spoke against God, or tore up a Christian leaflet given to you, may be the day you finally refused Christ. But you may yet be born again. Christ has done His utmost for you. He left heaven, coming to this earth in the form of a helpless baby. His express mission was to go to the cross. Far greater than any work of demonstrating power over the devil, disease, disaster or death, was His work of carrying the guilt of us all. Few in ancient history are known to us today, but all are known to God. We read of thousands of millions alive today, but God took the sin of every continent and country, and each man and woman, laying it on Jesus. The Bible says, 'All of us, like sheep, have strayed away. We have left God's paths to follow our own. Yet the LORD laid on him the sins of us all.'[24]

Let me illustrate this vital aspect of the Christian message.

Quite a few years ago, I used to be a teacher in a boys' secondary school. It was a unique school. I really enjoyed teaching there. It was in the days when there was still corporal punishment in most schools.

One day, in a particular class, I was being questioned by some boys. They were asking me about my Christian beliefs, and I remember explaining to them that I really did believe that Jesus had died to pay for our sins. After the lesson, an Indian boy, a pleasant character, came up to me and asked, 'Sir, how could Christ die for our sins?' Then later he said, 'I don't see how He could pay for my sins as I wasn't born.'

I explained how that with God there is no time. He can see the past, the present and the future, and He looked forward in time to see us and He took our sin and laid it on Christ. He actually bore the punishment for the wrong we had done so we could be forgiven.

He said, 'I can't believe that,' and we continued discussing things for about twenty-five minutes. It was all very amicable.

It would have been the end of the incident, except that about three weeks later I was teaching and he was in the class again, but this time was misbehaving. I repeatedly warned him as I told him to behave. However, he carried on. At the end of the lesson, there was an incident with a boy seated next to him, so I told the troublemaker to come to the front. 'Do you deserve to be slippered?' I asked. I had a slipper, which I used as a punishment for the boys. He replied, 'Well, I suppose I do, sir.' Suddenly, I remembered that this was the very lad who had asked me, 'How could Christ die for our sins?' So, instead of punishing him, I said, 'You have done wrong, but instead of me slippering you, I'm going to pass the slipper over to you. I'll bend over and you can slipper me as hard as I would have punished you.'

Well, of course, he and the class were delighted at the thought of this. I bent over and he took the slipper and he really did whack me right on the 'seat of learning'! Then I stood up, turned to him and said, 'Look, you did wrong, you deserved to be punished, but I took your punishment in your place. Do you remember that question of a few weeks before? How could Christ die for our sin? In a much greater way when Jesus Christ was on the cross He didn't just take our slippering; He took our sin and all the consequences of it, and He took the punishment so that we could be set free and forgiven.'

Raising Christ from the dead was God's seal on the work of paying the penalty for sin, which Jesus had done on the cross. Now to each person who will turn to Christ, God offers forgiveness, new birth, new life, and His everlasting presence.

A mischievous boy went up to a villager in Yorkshire, with a bird in his hand. 'Sir,' he asked, 'is this bird dead or alive?'

The wise man thought. 'If I say it's alive the boy will clench his hand and crush the bird to death. If, however, I say it's dead, the boy will open his hand and let the bird fly away free.'

The man gave his considered answer: 'Whether that bird is dead or alive depends entirely upon you.'

So too, you have the responsibility: either to reject or to receive Christ. If you will turn from your sin and trust Jesus to forgive and live in you, then God will work a wonderful miracle within you. Spiritual, eternal life will be yours. You will be part of God's family for ever. If you refuse Him, your heart will harden further against God, and who knows how long God will continue to give you opportunities to trust Him?

Thirdly note, this is the *moment* to be born again. God makes no promises about tomorrow. Life is short and uncertain. Even if we have a heart still ticking and a mind still functioning, there is no guarantee that He will still be speaking to us or that our hearts will be inclined towards Him, 'Indeed, the "right time" is now. Today is the day of salvation.'[25]

There is a legend about the devil interviewing for a junior. He had shortlisted three demons. To each he asked, 'What would you do to prevent people trusting Christ?' The first replied that he would say that there is no God, and the second that there is no judgement. The devil was not content with either of these, feeling that they were not sufficiently convincing. Then he asked the third the same question. The reply came: 'I would tell them that there is no hurry.' This demon understood well the urgency of God's call to humanity. He was taken on instantly.

Procrastination is the thief of time, and of eternity. It is well said that the road to hell is paved with good intentions. I urge you today to take the most important step in your life. Ask God to forgive your sin, and ask Him to be your Lord and Saviour today. If you are genuinely repentant and trusting, then God will give you a new birth and spiritual life. He will lift you to a new plane of life and begin the process of making you into the person you were created to be.

> *But to all who believed him and accepted him, he gave the right to become children of God. They are reborn – not with a physical birth resulting from human passion or plan, but a birth that comes from God.*[26]

NOTES

1. John 1:12
2. Genesis 1:10,12,18,21,25
3. Genesis 2:18
4. Genesis 1:26; 2:7
5. Genesis 3:9
6. Matthew 10:15; 11:21–24
7. Galatians 5:19–21
8. 1 Timothy 1:15
9. Matthew 9:13
10. Richard Cecil (ed.). *The Works of the Rev. John Newton* (New York: Robert Garter Co., 1844), Volume 1, p.95ff.

11. C.S. Lewis, *Surprised by Joy* (London: Collins, Fount Paperbacks, 1955), p.179. Used with permission

12. Acts 9:11

13. Luke 9:23

14. Acts 9:15–16

15. 2 Timothy 3:12

16. Matthew 5:5

17. See Ephesians 1:13–14; 2 Corinthians 1:21; 5:5

18. John 3:3

19. Galatians 4:4–6

20. See John 3:1–3, NKJV

21. John 3:4–8

22. 1 Corinthians 2:2–16

23. John 3:19

24. Isaiah 53:6

25. 2 Corinthians 6:2

26. 1 John 1:12–13

7.

Why I Believe Jesus is the Only Way to God

Jesus said: 'I am the way, the truth, and the life. No one can come to the Father except through me.'[1]

The sun was riding high in a Mexican sky. Hundreds of people were gathered at the foot of the ancient pyramid. It was AD 1300. Since early morning they had been waiting anxiously for the great event. By the sundial, it was almost time. Suddenly a great shout arose for, as they gazed as far as they could see across the lake, they saw a little boat coming their way. As the boat approached, they could discern the figure of a young Indian, handsome, athletic, in the prime of life. As this young Indian slowly paddled his boat to the sandy beach, the jewels on his magnificent garment glistened in the sunlight. Slowly and deliberately, with a deadpan expression, he made his way through a path that the crowd gladly made for him, toward the pyramid, while garlands of tropical flowers were thrown for his path. Scores knelt and cried. 'Take my sins … Take my sins … Take my sins' or 'Remember me … Remember me … Remember me.'

Just as he reached the stone steps leading to the summit, priests came and quickly stripped him of all his garments. Blue, white, red and yellow paint was put on his body. After preparation and more prayers, alone he slowly climbed the 100 steps. The crowd waited anxiously, breathlessly, excitedly. At last, he reached the top. Out of nowhere stepped six priests ... four gripped each limb of his body and quickly bent him over a convex stone. A fifth held his head. A sixth priest had a long, curved, jewelled knife, sharp as a razor's edge. Looking toward the small temple erected on the top of the pyramid, and gazing at the face of the stone-carved god, the Indian chanted a few syllables. Like a flash, the knife pierced the heart of the young man. A skilful twist and the heart was out.

Each priest reached madly into the place where the heart had been and sprinkled his face with the warm blood. The heart, still palpitating, was rubbed over the face of the image. The twitching body was thrown, head first, over the side of the pyramid. A mad scramble followed. Knives flashed. Each person scrambled to get a piece of flesh to take home for use in a 'communion service' that would bring added blessing.

The sun was sinking over the western horizon when the crowd melted in the distance. Each felt that his sins were forgiven and that the evils that had come upon himself or his family were now atoned for. This was not an unusual scene to the ancient Aztecs, for it happened somewhere in their domain every day. They had eighteen months of twenty days each on their calendar, and each day there were many gods and goddesses to receive sacrifices. Thus 20,000 human beings a year were slaughtered on the altars of ancient Mexico.

These ancient people engaged in constant warfare to get their sacrificial victims from neighbouring tribes and nations, for the victim sacrificed must be innocent of the particular sins and evils that were to be atoned for. Thus he must come from outside the realm. He must be young and without blemish. For many months before the sacrifice he was carefully trained and was treated in many respects as a god. He was the substitute bearing the sins of the people.[2]

So began one of the American evangelist Billy Graham's early, graphic sermons.

We humans are incurably religious. Perverted and perverse though religious practices may be, in every part of the globe people 'worship'.

The recent growth in cults and eastern religions has been phenomenal. But this is nothing new. Ever since Cain killed Abel at the beginning of time, there has been a basic divide between those who hope that their works and behaviour will please and placate their god, and those who have relied on and rested in the work of a substitute to cleanse them from sin and bring them to God.

Sincerity may be the hallmark of many religious people, but that is not enough. A sincere person taking poison instead of medicine, genuinely believing that the dose will cure them, is not thereby immune from that chemical's fatal effect. The apostle Paul said the same thing when he wrote:

I know what enthusiasm they [the religious people of his day] have for God, but it is misdirected zeal. For they don't understand God's way of making people right with himself. Refusing to accept God's way, they cling to their own way of getting right with God by trying to keep the law.[3]

From the beginning, God provided a way for people to have fellowship with Him. Rather than an idea of an evolution of religion (starting with a fear of spirits, then progressing to polytheism, followed by monotheism until the present stage of familiarity with God), God has actually stepped into His creation and revealed Himself to us.

At first there were shadowy ideas and prophetic pictures and practices in this revelation. This culminated in the coming of Christ, the promised Messiah. He, by His life, death and resurrection, put the finishing strokes to the background picture of all that had been anticipated throughout the Old Testament period.

Humanity's many methods of groping and grovelling its way back to God are in vain. God has taken the initiative and condescended to reach us.

Most religions believe in the existence of a supreme being, with whom they hope, by various means, to make contact, if not in this world then in a world or existence to come. Very often their life's endeavours are all for that very purpose.

There will be elements of truth in any religion that survives. There will be devotees to particular religious systems who will speak of the help they feel they have received from their religion. Some of that may be humanly inexplicable and appear supernatural.

Let us be quite clear that whatever the differences in belief, the real Christian will want to show love and compassion to people, whatever their religious views. After all, it was while we were enemies of God that Christ died for us. Jesus' parable of the Good Samaritan is as applicable for today as for any other generation. Christians will find that there is profound disagreement with many of the teachings of systems that demote or exclude Christ. But the Christian will want to obey the Jesus who said:

> *You have heard the law that says, 'Love your neighbour' and*
> *hate your enemy. But I say, love your enemies! Pray for those who*

*persecute you! In that way, you will be acting as true children of
your Father in heaven. For he gives his sunlight to both the evil
and the good, and he sends rain on the just and the unjust alike.
If you love only those who love you, what reward is there for that?
Even corrupt tax collectors do that much. If you are kind only to
your friends, how are you different from anyone else? Even pagans
do that.*[4]

Jesus taught the duty of His followers was to give food to the
hungry, drink to the thirsty, loving care to the 'stranger', clothing to
the naked, attention to the sick and timely visits to the prisoners.[5]

When I am asked, 'Haven't more wars been fought over
religion than anything else?' my mind goes back to these passages
in the Bible. How can a real Christian fight with someone simply
because there are religious differences? Sadly, just as the cloak of
Christ was gambled for at the cross, and then presumably worn
by somebody to whom it did not belong, so too, the name of
Jesus has often been taken by those to whom it does not belong,
who have 'worn' it and abused it. If, going directly against your
instructions, I murdered in your name, are you to blame? Surely
not! A Christian will feel deeply that all need to come to Christ,
but they are not going to fight someone who doesn't. Rather, they
will want to love that person all the more.

God has revealed Himself to the world. He has clearly shown
that the picture of God at the top of a high hill with various routes
up to Him, is absolutely wrong. It may be taught in Religious
Education lessons in school, and even in church pulpits, but it is
not taught anywhere in the Bible. God, who loves so much, has
gone to great lengths to show us the only way of escape from sin
and to enjoy Him eternally. And this way is open to all.

There are five reasons for believing that there is only one way
to God.

God's character

There is always a tendency for humans to make God in our own image. We are small and full of corruption compared with the great and holy God. So many religions set rules which they feel must be obeyed if people are ever to reach God. But is God really that petty? If God is God, then He is infinitely greater than anything men or women can fully comprehend. The only hope is that God will Himself stoop to reach us. If I could fully understand Him, then God would not be God, and I would not be a mere mortal.

In wisdom, honour, glory and knowledge, God is infinitely superior to us. He is 'pure and cannot stand the sight of evil'.[6] He is called 'Holy, holy, holy'.[7] He has never grown accustomed to sin, nor trifled with it. The Ten Commandments are not only His commandments for us today, but also the expression of His character. He has never lied, stolen, coveted; He never spoke falsely.

That is why no sin will ever be allowed into heaven. At the very end of the Bible we read, 'Nothing evil will be allowed to enter, nor anyone who practices shameful idolatry and dishonesty – but only those whose names are written in the Lamb's Book of Life.'[8] Perhaps this is because if God allowed sin into His presence, soon there would be wars and rumours of war, hatred, and murder, and heaven would be as earth.

When John saw a vision of Jesus, we read that he 'fell at his feet as if [he] were dead'.[9] Those who feel they can attain God by their own efforts have a god who is too small.

The human condition

Spend too much time looking in a mirror and you may begin to wish you could not see yourself so clearly. Spend some time looking at God's honest portrayal of people in the Bible, and you will see how clearly God demonstrates that all are rebels before Him. In fact, God's Word has accurately been described as a mirror.[10]

The Bible's greatest characters are portrayed very honestly, 'warts and all'. Noah became a drunkard, Abraham and Sarah laughed at God's promise, Jacob deceived his own father and brother, Moses murdered, Samson squandered his strength on pagan women, David committed adultery, Solomon turned to folly, many of the kings of Israel and Judah were idolatrous, Peter denied Jesus, the disciples fled and Thomas doubted Him. So much for heroes! But we are all like them. 'For everyone has sinned; we all fall short of God's glorious standard.'[11]

Good intentions, New Year's resolutions or turning over new leaves all fail to improve our basic condition. We are plagued by wrong attitudes and deeds. God's verdict on all of us is identical: 'The Lord observed the extent of human wickedness on the earth, and he saw that everything they thought or imagined was consistently and totally evil.'[12]

It is impossible for us to lift ourselves to God, or bring God down to us. The holy God can have no dealing with sinful men and women. God is not sitting around a negotiating table waiting for us to improve our offer or promise obedience. As the hymn *Rock of Ages* puts it:

> *Not the labours of my hands*
> *Can fulfil God's law's demands,*
> *Could my zeal no respite know*
> *Could my tears for ever flow,*
> *All for sin could not atone,*
> *God must save and God alone.*[13]

The commonly held view of Christianity that it simply teaches us to improve ourselves, or that the 'good go up and the bad go down', is far from the truth of what the Bible teaches. For example, the Bible says:

> *God saved you by his grace when you believed. And you can't take credit for this; it is a gift from God. Salvation is not a reward for the good things we have done, so none of us can boast about it.*[14]

> *When God our Saviour revealed his kindness and love, he saved us, not because of the righteous things we had done, but because of his mercy. He washed away our sins, giving us a new birth and new life through the Holy Spirit. He generously poured out the Spirit upon us through Jesus Christ our Saviour.*[15]

> *I [Jesus] have come to call not those who think they are righteous, but those who know they are sinners.*[16]

This is not flattering to our human ego, but it is like balm to the person who realistically sees themselves not as others see them, but as God sees them.

The advert showed a boy in what looked like a fine white shirt, until he compared it to a Brand X white shirt! I may be all right compared with some of the people whose deeds hit the headlines, but contrasted with the purity of Christ, I am guilty. But it is for such as me that Jesus came to save.

Thomas Bilney was a young student of Canon Law at Oxford University in 1516. Deeply religious, he was nevertheless conscious of sin in his life. His priest advised him to increasingly pray and fast, but it all seemed to no avail for this devotee. Erasmus' Greek New Testament had been declared illegal by the Roman Catholic Church, but despite that he bought a copy of this new book and secretly read it. He avidly devoured the Gospels, Acts and Epistles until he came to Paul's first letter to Timothy in which he read: 'This is a trustworthy saying, and everyone should accept it: "Christ Jesus came into the world to save sinners" – and I am the worst of them all.'[17] Bilney thought, 'How can Paul be the worst of sinners? I am!' Then he realised that if Paul was the worst of sinners and yet Jesus had died for him, so Christ must also have died for Thomas Bilney. Confessing nothing except his sin, Bilney claimed the forgiveness that Christ died to procure. In an instant, Bilney's guilty conscience was eased and he felt inexpressible joy.

'We contribute nothing to our salvation except our sin,' said Archbishop William Temple. But that is what we all have, yet God willingly takes it from those who give it to Him.

Jesus' claims

Tolerance is not necessarily a virtue. It depends what issue one is tolerant towards. Intolerance is not necessarily wrong. I am intolerant towards terrorists, murderers, rapists and the like. Christ was deeply intolerant towards error. His harshest words were reserved not for the problem drinkers or the immoral (though of course He deplored such wrongs), but for the religious hypocrites of the day. The offer of eternal life is open to all, no matter what sex, age, state of health, colour, class, creed, upbringing or lifestyle.

It is ironic how those who will not submit themselves to the law of God invent other sins by which they judge society. Political correctness appears more important than the flagrant denial of the Ten Commandments. Jesus, without fear, spoke out against, and touched the nerve of, our sinfulness. Read for example his blistering denunciation of hypocrisy.

> *The teachers of religious law and the Pharisees are the official interpreters of the law of Moses. So practice and obey*

whatever they tell you, but don't follow their example. For they don't practice what they teach. They crush people with unbearable religious demands and never lift a finger to ease the burden. Everything they do is for show. On their arms they wear extra wide prayer boxes with Scripture verses inside, and they wear robes with extra long tassels. And they love to sit at the head table at banquets and in the seats of honour in the synagogues ...

What sorrow awaits you teachers of religious law and you Pharisees. Hypocrites! For you cross land and sea to make one convert, and then you turn that person into twice the child of hell you yourselves are! ...

What sorrow awaits you teachers of religious law and you Pharisees. Hypocrites! For you are so careful to clean the outside of the cup and the dish, but inside you are filthy - full of greed and self-indulgence! You blind Pharisee! First wash the inside of the cup and the dish, and then the outside will become clean, too.

What sorrow awaits you teachers of religious law and you Pharisees. Hypocrites! For you are like whitewashed tombs – beautiful on the outside but filled on the inside with dead people's bones and all sorts of impurity. Outwardly you look like righteous people, but inwardly your hearts are filled with hypocrisy and lawlessness.

What sorrow awaits you teachers of religious law and you Pharisees. Hypocrites! For you build tombs for the prophets your ancestors killed, and you decorate the monuments of the godly people your ancestors destroyed. Then you say, 'If we had lived in the days of our ancestors, we would never have joined them in killing the prophets.' But in saying that, you testify against yourselves that you are indeed the descendants of those who murdered the prophets.[18]

Who would feel good enough to stand before God's all-seeing gaze? Yet our very condition is the one with which He came to deal. He said, 'Healthy people don't need a doctor – sick people do.'[19] His express mission on earth was to die so that He could be the means whereby God could forgive sins. He was born to do just that. It is the work of God, and evidence that Jesus is Himself God, that He could wash away the guilt of ordinary men and women.

If nobody is good enough for God, or able to climb up to Him, then our only hope is that He would come down to us, to forgive the sin and remove the barrier that separates us from Him. That is exactly what Christ has done.

He set His face steadfastly to go to Jerusalem where He would die, bearing in His own body the sin of us all.

All of us, like sheep, have strayed away. We have left God's paths to follow our own. Yet the Lord laid on him the sins of us all.[20]

Christ suffered for our sins once for all time. He never sinned, but he died for sinners to bring you safely home to God. He suffered physical death, but he was raised to life in the Spirit.[21]

He personally carried our sins in his body on the cross so that we can be dead to sin and live for what is right. By his wounds you are healed.[22]

But God showed his great love for us by sending Christ to die for us while we were still sinners.[23]

Imagine a person drowning at sea. Standing on the seashore are people such as Buddha, Mohammed, Moses, the gurus and a host of other religious leaders. All are shouting instructions to the desperate man. Each tells him how to swim. Each piece of advice is contradicting the others. In contrast, Jesus dives in to rescue the person. In so doing, Christ gives His own life.

In reality this is the difference between Christianity and other religions. Rather than us striving to reach God, Christ came to rescue us. We need to trust in Him, not try our best. Instead of 'being' and 'doing', we should rely on who Christ is and what He has done.

That is why Jesus could say, 'I am the way, the truth, and the life. No one can come to the Father except through me' and: 'Yes, I am the gate. Those who come in through me will be saved. They will come and go freely and will find good pastures.'[24]

These are not the words of a mere prophet, or we would accuse Jesus of megalomania or delusion. There is an exclusiveness about Christ, or as someone put it: 'If all religions are right, then Jesus is right, and if Jesus is right, then all other religions are wrong. Right?' Christ is the only way to God, because He came from God to remove all that cuts us off and keeps us from God.

Peter, the apostle and early preacher, proclaimed, 'There is salvation in no one else! God has given no other name under heaven by which we must be saved.'[25]

Paul wrote, 'For there is only one God and one Mediator who can reconcile God and humanity – the man Christ Jesus.'[26]

In Athens at the famous 'Speakers' Corner' called the Areopagus, Paul said:

> *God overlooked people's ignorance about these things in earlier times, but now he commands everyone everywhere to repent of their sins and turn to him. For he has set a day for judging the world with justice by the man he has appointed, and he proved to everyone who this is by raising him from the dead.*[27]

Christ is not an option to be selected or rejected, but the only way to God, the one who should be received as Lord and Saviour. If there were any other means whereby sin could be forgiven, God would not have allowed Jesus to die so brutally under the crushing load of sin.

And if Jesus was anything less than God manifest in the flesh, then God would not have raised Him from the dead. The American evangelist, R.A. Torrey wrote:

> *When Jesus died, He died as my representative, and I died in Him; when He arose, He rose as my representative, and I arose in Him; when He ascended up on high and took His place at the right hand of the Father in the glory, He ascended as my representative and I ascended in Him, and today I am seated in Christ with God in the heavenlies. I look at the cross of Christ, and I know that atonement has been made for my sins; I look at the open sepulchre and the risen and ascended Lord, and I know the atonement has been accepted. There no longer remains a single sin on me, no matter how many or how great my sins may have been.*[28]

The Bible says Jesus 'was handed over to die because of our sins, and he was raised to life to make us right with God'.[29]

For three days, as Jesus' body lay in the tomb, a watching and waiting world could have wondered if Christ's death was sufficient to pay for the sins of the world. When Jesus rose and the stone rolled away from the tomb, no one needed to doubt. Jesus was risen; God could now live in the hearts of those who would believe on Him.

It is possible to visit the tombs of many influential world leaders, both political and religious. All die. Only Jesus' tomb is empty. Only He rose from the dead. This is the great sign that

He is trustworthy. In fact the Jews asked Jesus what sign He gave since He claimed God was His Father: 'Jesus replied. "Destroy this temple, and in three days I will raise it up." … when Jesus said "this temple", he meant his own body.'[30]

On another occasion Jesus said:

> … the only sign I will give them [this generation] is the sign of the prophet Jonah. For as Jonah was in the belly of the great fish for three days and three nights, so will the Son of Man be in the heart of the earth for three days and three nights.[31]

God is willing to declare men and women righteous on the basis of Jesus' death and resurrection for them. No other way has ever been provided.

The gospel's call

The cross of Christ as the means for us to be brought back into fellowship with God was not an afterthought of God. It is, in fact, the theme of the Old and New Testaments.

Jesus' death was anticipated

At the beginning of time, immediately after Adam and Eve had sinned, God made a specific promise. To the serpent God spoke: 'And I will cause hostility between you and the woman, and between your offspring and her offspring. He will strike your head, and you will strike his heel.'[32]

Note that only the offspring of *the woman* is mentioned. So early in the Bible there is the first hint of the virgin birth. Indeed, Christ struck the head of the serpent Satan, as He overcame the great weapons of sin and death by dying and rising again.

Seven hundred years before Jesus' birth, Isaiah the prophet wrote:

He was despised and rejected – a man of sorrows, acquainted with deepest grief. We turned our backs on him and looked the other way. He was despised, and we did not care. Yet it was our weaknesses he carried; it was our sorrows that weighed him down. And we thought his troubles were a punishment from God, a punishment for his own sins! But he was pierced for our rebellion, crushed for our sins. He was beaten so we could be whole. He was whipped so we could be healed. All of us, like sheep, have strayed away. We have left God's paths to follow our own. Yet the LORD laid on him the sins of us all. He was oppressed and treated harshly, yet he never said a word. He was led like a lamb to the slaughter. And as a sheep is silent before the shearers, he did not open his mouth. Unjustly condemned, he was led away. No one cared that he died without descendants, that his life was cut short in midstream. But he was struck down for the rebellion of my people. He had done no wrong and had never deceived anyone. But he was buried like a criminal; he was put in a rich man's grave.[33]

Earlier, David in the Psalms had written prophetically the words and work of Christ as He suffered as a servant atoning for sin.

My God, my God, why have you abandoned me? … Everyone who sees me mocks me. They sneer and shake their heads, saying, 'Is this the one who relies on the LORD? Then let the LORD save him! If the LORD loves him so much, let the LORD rescue him!' … My life is poured out like water, and all my bones are out of joint. My heart is like wax, melting within me.[34]

Not only through prophecy, but also pictures, every obedient Israelite who lived before the Messiah (or Christ) came, eagerly anticipated His coming. Conscious of guilt, a Jew would take a spotless male lamb to the priest, who would lay his hand, along with that of the sinner, on the head of the lamb. Then the lamb would die, its blood shed as a sacrifice and substitute for sin. Every time the ritual was performed it was a shadowy prefiguring of Christ dying. Jesus was to die as the sacrifice and substitute for our sin.

At the time of Jesus' birth, the angel said to Joseph 'you are to name him Jesus, for he will save his people from their sins'.[35] The name 'Jesus' means Saviour.

Then Jesus Himself anticipated His own death. He said repeatedly, 'My time has not yet come', until the time of His crucifixion when He said, 'the hour has come'.[36] Jesus said, 'For even the Son of Man came not to be served but to serve others and to give his life as a ransom for many' and, 'The Son of Man is going to be betrayed into the hands of his enemies. He will be killed, but on the third day he will be raised from the dead.'[37]

Even in the glorious moment when Jesus was transfigured we read that He spoke about the death that He was about to accomplish.[38] Jesus asked His disciples: 'Who do people say that the Son of Man is?' Apparently there were various suggestions, some thinking that He was John the Baptist others, Elijah, Jeremiah, or one of the prophets. When asked, 'But who do you say I am?' Peter answered resoundingly, 'You are the Messiah, the Son of the living God.' As the disciples clearly understood who He was, Jesus immediately explained His mission, so we read: 'From then on Jesus began to tell his disciples plainly that it was necessary for him to go to Jerusalem, and that he would suffer many terrible things at the hands of the elders, the leading priests, and the teachers of religious law. He would be killed, but on the third day he would be raised from the dead.'[39]

Later Jesus warned again of all that would happen: 'The Son of Man is going to be betrayed into the hands of his enemies.

He will be killed, but on the third day he will be raised from the dead.'[40]

Jesus was not caught unawares or taken by surprise when He was betrayed, arrested, manhandled and crucified. Immediately after sin entered our world, God revealed His plan and gave His promise. Thousands of years later, as men and women did their worst, God gave His best and fulfilled the anticipation of the ages.

Jesus' death was accomplished

When Jesus called out on the cross, 'It is finished' this was not the defeated moan of a dying man, but the cry of His completed work.[41] The Greek word used here actually means 'completely complete' or 'perfectly perfect'.

Many things in this world are not finished. We have a famous 'unfinished symphony', we live amongst unfinished plans, books, architecture and dreams. Jesus at the age of 33 finished the work He was born to do.

F.W. Farrar, in his book *The Life of Christ*, describes the awful physical trauma of execution by crucifixion:

> *For indeed a death by crucifixion seems to include all that pain and death can have of horrible and ghastly – dizziness, cramp, thirst, starvation, sleeplessness, traumatic fever, tetanus, shame, publicity of shame, long continuance of torment, horror of anticipation, mortification of untended wounds – all intensified just up to the point at which they can be endured at all, but all stopping just short of the point which would give to the sufferer the relief of unconsciousness.*
>
> *The unnatural position made every movement painful; the lacerated veins and crushed tendons throbbed with incessant anguish; the wounds, inflamed by exposure, gradually gangrened; the arteries – especially at the head and stomach – became swollen*

*and oppressed with surcharged blood; and while each variety of
misery went on gradually increasing, there was added to them
the intolerable pang of a burning and raging thirst; and all
these physical complications caused an internal excitement and
anxiety, which made the prospect of death itself – of death, the
unknown enemy, at whose approach man usually shudders most
– bear the aspect of a delicious and exquisite release.*[42]

Humankind did its worst against Jesus. And out of love for us, so
did God the Father: 'it was the LORD's will to crush him and cause
him to suffer … the LORD makes his life a guilt offering'.[43] Jesus
took God's anger and judgement against sin on Himself as He
hung on the cross.

God laid on Him all the world's sin. The worst deeds that
hit the headlines as well as the everyday wrongs of us all were
compacted on to the pure and holy Jesus. Like a railway yard's van
with its brakes fixed, standing still as the weight of all the goods
wagons are shunted on to it, so Christ stood under the crushing
load of the sin of the world. He paid the price of every last wrong
thought, word and deed, past, present and future. Sins of wrong
attitudes and actions, of things remembered by us or forgotten,
were all on Christ. He took the punishment from God.[44] At this
point came the *coup de grâce*. As well as Jesus bearing all sin, He
took the consequences of it too. Jesus was cut off from His Father.
Our sin separated Him from His Father and caused God's face to
be turned from Him. The grief this caused Christ was expressed
in His agonizing cry from the cross: 'My God, my God, why have
you abandoned me?'[45]

Yet all this was in fulfilment of the plan of the loving God: 'For
God loved the world so much that he gave his one and only Son,
so that everyone who believes in him will not perish but have
eternal life.'[46]

Jesus' death must be appropriated

God's greatest offer to each individual is that He will forgive any who come to Him. God is not in a hurry to judge, though judge He must. The door of Noah's ark remained open seven days as an act of invitation to all to enter. Then God finally closed the door. The Israelites marched for seven days around the walls of Jericho before they eventually fell.

In contrast, the prodigal son's father, in Jesus' parable, ran to meet and greet his returning child. It is all a picture of a God who is slow to judge but in a hurry to save those who will turn in faith to Him, a God who is patient. We read: 'He does not want anyone to be destroyed, but wants everyone to repent.'[47]

Martin Luther, the German reformer, received a letter from a distressed monk. In his reply, Luther wrote:

> *Learn to know Christ and Him crucified. Learn to sing to Him and say, 'Lord Jesus, you are my righteousness, I am your sin; you took on you what was mine, yet set on me what was yours. You became what you were not, that I might become what I was not.'*[48]

That is it. Jesus' work can be appropriated by an act of faith, a decision to believe. When a couple stand at the front of a church and make vows committing themselves to each other in marriage, their words change their whole status before God, each other and society. So, too, if we will become followers of Christ, words that confess sin and express our trust in His finished work need to be framed in the mind or spoken audibly as the expression of an enduring commitment.

Even now, you could ask Jesus to be your personal Lord and Saviour.

The Christian's certainty

I have asked many people if they are sure of going to heaven when they die. Usually their hope is based on the false view that their deeds are good enough to grant them a place in heaven, forgetting that God sees into all parts of our minds and lives. Jesus warned all such when, in the Sermon on the Mount, He said:

> *Not everyone who calls out to me, 'Lord! Lord!' will enter the Kingdom of Heaven. Only those who actually do the will of my Father in heaven will enter. On judgment day many will say to me, 'Lord! Lord! We prophesied in your name and cast out demons in your name and performed many miracles in your name.' But I will reply, 'I never knew you. Get away from me, you who break God's laws.'*[49]

In contrast, Christians know for sure that instead of the hell they deserve they are guaranteed heaven as a free gift from a loving God.

Look at some of these promises in the Bible, which speak of the Christian's certainty:

> *And anyone who believes in God's Son has eternal life. Anyone who doesn't obey the Son will never experience eternal life but remains under God's angry judgment.*[50]

> *I tell you the truth, those who listen to my message and believe in God who sent me have eternal life. They will never be condemned for their sins, but they have already passed from death into life.*[51]

> *I tell you the truth, anyone who believes has eternal life.*[52]

I have written this to you who believe in the name of the Son of God, so that you may know you have eternal life.[53]

So we are always confident, even though we know that as long as we live in these bodies we are not at home with the Lord … Yes, we are fully confident, and we would rather be away from these earthly bodies, for then we will be at home with the Lord.[54]

But we are citizens of heaven, where the Lord Jesus Christ lives. And we are eagerly waiting for him to return as our Saviour.[55]

If you confess with your mouth that Jesus is Lord and believe in your heart that God raised him from the dead, you will be saved. For it is by believing in your heart that you are made right with God, and it is by confessing with your mouth that you are saved. As the Scriptures tell us, 'Anyone who trusts in him will never be disgraced.' … For 'Everyone who calls on the name of the LORD *will be saved.'*[56]

Christian experience is not 'pie in the sky when you die' but rather 'steak on the plate while you wait'.

A Christian actually knows God in the here and now. He is real to every believer. Christ has become a friend and very present help to the Christian. He who 'did not spare even his own Son but gave him up for us all' also gives us all the things we need.[57]

It is a wonderful experience to know that now 'there is no condemnation' because we 'belong to Christ Jesus'[58] Jesus has dealt with the Christian's past; He is dealing with their present, and He guarantees their future. This very moment, will you trust Jesus as your Lord and Saviour and as the one who will reconcile you to God forever?

NOTES

1. John 14:6
2. Billy Graham, *Calling Youth to Christ* (Grand Rapids, MI: Zondervan, 1947)
3. Romans 10:2–3
4. Matthew 5:43–47
5. Matthew 25:31–46
6. Habakkuk 1:13
7. Isaiah 6:3; Revelation 4:8
8. Revelation 21:27
9. Revelation 1:17
10. James 1:22–25; 2 Corinthians 3:18
11. Romans 3:23
12. Genesis 6:5
13. 'Rock of Ages', A. Toplady, 1740–78
14. Ephesians 2:8–9
15. Titus 3:4–6
16. Matthew 9:13
17. 1 Timothy 1:15
18. Matthew 23:2–6,15,25–31
19. Matthew 9:12
20. Isaiah 53:6
21. 1 Peter 3:18
22. 1 Peter 2:24
23. Romans 5:8
24. John 14:6; 10:9
25. Act 4:12
26. 1 Timothy 2:5
27. Acts 17:30–31
28. R.A. Torrey, *The Bible and Its Christ* (New Jersey: Fleming H. Revell), pp.107,108
29. Romans 4:25

30. John 2:18–21

31. Matthew 12:39–40

32. Genesis 3:15

33. Isaiah 53:3–9

34. Psalm 22:1,7–8,14

35. Matthew 1:21

36. John 2:4; 17:1

37. Mark 10:45; Matthew 17:22–23

38. See Luke 9:31

39. Matthew 16:13–16, 21

40. Matthew 17:22–23

41. John 19:30

42. F.W. Farrar, *The Life of Christ* (London: Dutton, Dovar, Cassell & Co, 1897), p.440

43. Isaiah 53:10, NIV

44. Isaiah 53:4

45. Matthew 27:46; Mark 15:34

46. John 3:16

47. 2 Peter 3:9

48. Theodore G. Tappert (ed.), *The Library of Christian Classics*, 'Letters of Spiritual Counsel', Vol. XVIII (London: SCM, 1955), p.110

49. Matthew 7:21–23

50. John 3:36

51. John 5:24

52. John 6:47

53. 1 John 5:13

54. 2 Corinthians 5:6–8

55. Philippians 3:20

56. Romans 10:9–11,13

57. Romans 8:32

58. Romans 8:1

8.

Will You Believe?

Jesus said: 'unless you are born again, you cannot see the Kingdom of God … You must be born again.'[1]

Today when you hear his voice, don't harden your hearts.[2]

Having sought to explain various aspects of the Christian gospel, as well as briefly looking at a tiny tip of the iceberg of evidence, what will you do about Jesus?

The claims of Christ are such that they demand a response. The Bible asks, 'How much longer will you waver, hobbling between two opinions? If the LORD is God, follow him! But if Baal is God, then follow him!'[3] Baal was a pagan god, symbolizing all that comes between us and the true and living God. We read, 'choose today whom you will serve'.[4]

The most important task in life is to make sure that you are at peace with God. God's Word, the Bible, tells us how this is possible, and why it is necessary.

In this summary of the Bible's teaching about how you may find peace with God, see if you can go along with each step. Then I suggest you pray a prayer similar to the one at the end of the chapter. It will be a deliberate act of faith.

We read in the Bible: 'Yet to all who received him, to those who believed in his name, he gave the right to become children of God'.[5]

We must receive Jesus as our Sin-bearer

We have seen that when Jesus died on the cross, God laid all our sins on Him. Therefore we need to receive Christ as Sin-bearer. We must confess to God – that is, agree with Him – that we are guilty of sin, make a positive decision to turn away from that sin, and ask Him to pardon us. The Bible says:

All of us, like sheep, have strayed away. We have left God's paths to follow our own. Yet the LORD laid on him the sins of us all.[6]

He personally carried our sins in his body on the cross[7]

We must receive Jesus as our Saviour

Jesus not only died; three days later, He rose from the dead. As Saviour, Jesus both forgives past wrongs and gives us strength to live new lives. Asking Him into our lives means taking Him as the one who will give us power over sin day by day. The Holy Spirit (God Himself) will live within us. The Bible says:

Therefore he is able, once and forever, to save those who come to God through him. He lives forever to intercede with God on their behalf.[8]

Since he himself has gone through suffering and testing, he is able to help us when we are being tested.[9]

Don't you realize that your body is the temple of the Holy Spirit, who lives in you and was given to you by God? You do not belong to yourself, for God bought you with a high price. So you must honour God with your body.[10]

We must receive Jesus as our Sovereign

Trusting Jesus is not only asking Him to wipe clean the past, but also to take charge of the present and the future. He will guide our lives as we serve and obey Him in everything. The Bible says:

Christ died and rose again for this very purpose – to be Lord both of the living and of the dead.[11]

[Jesus said:] 'If any of you wants to be my follower, you must turn from your selfish ways, take up your cross daily, and follow me.'[12]

[God] commands everyone everywhere to repent of their sins and turn to him.[13]

This means we must be willing to turn from sin, and turn to Christ. As we do, God turns to us – He works a miracle in us.

Will you now pray, asking Jesus to be your personal Sin-bearer, Saviour and Sovereign? In the moment that you sincerely trust Christ, He will forgive you and make you His forever. The Bible says:

However, those the Father has given me will come to me, and I will never reject them.[14]

I give them eternal life, and they will never perish. No one can snatch them away from me.[15]

I have written this to you who believe … that you may know you have eternal life.[16]

Many have found that praying with similar words to the ones below has helped them in the act of putting their trust in Jesus. Will you pray like this now?

Heavenly Father, I confess my sin to You and want to repent of it. Please forgive me. I trust Christ as my Sin-bearer, my Saviour and my Sovereign. Help me grow to become a strong Christian. Thank You for loving me. I pray in Jesus' name. Amen.

If you have prayed this and, as far as you are able, have meant what you have said, then you are a new creation in Christ, you have been born again of the Spirit. It will be helpful to write down the date you prayed like this, and to tell someone of your newfound faith and life in Christ. He has promised abundant life from now on, life with purpose, direction and meaning.

This is the first day of a new life ...

NOTES

1. John 3:3,7
2. Hebrews 3:7–8
3. 1 Kings 18:21
4. Joshua 24:15
5. John 1:12, NIV
6. Isaiah 53:6
7. 1 Peter 2:24
8. Hebrews 7:25
9. Hebrews 2:18
10. 1 Corinthians 6:19–20
11. Romans 14:9
12. Luke 9:23
13. Acts 17:30
14. John 6:37
15. John 10:28
16. 1 John 5:13

9.

When You Believe

This means that anyone who belongs to Christ has become a new person. The old life is gone; a new life has begun![1]

If you have prayed the prayer at the end of chapter 8 and meant it and, as far as you can tell, have genuinely repented and believed in Jesus, then you will want to start to live for Him who has promised His new life in you. The Lord wants us to be holy, because He is holy.[2] God doesn't ask us to do anything without revealing the way and providing the means. We read, 'By his divine power, God has given us everything we need for living a godly life. We have received all of this by coming to know him, the one who called us to himself by means of his marvellous glory and excellence.'[3] Jesus never promised that the Christian life would be easy. As we saw earlier, Jesus said, 'If any of you wants to be my follower, you must turn from your selfish ways, take up your cross daily, and follow me' and Paul knew that 'everyone who wants to live a godly life in Christ Jesus will suffer persecution'.[4] However, there is a wonderful joy and peace that can be experienced only by the Christian.

Trust and obey,
For there's no other way

To be happy in Jesus,
But to trust and obey.[5]

Christian living is an adventure in which God wants your joy to be full and your steps to be directed by Him. Peter said that when we believe in Him we are filled with an inexpressible and glorious joy.[6]

Christianity is not a club, hobby, or sideline. It is a lifelong, developing relationship with the loving God whose desire is towards the individual believer. He wants to mould and make the Christian into somebody who is Christ-like.[7] It is God's desire that every believer in Christ will become ever more like Him, exhibiting the fruit of the Holy Spirit in their lives: love, joy, peace, patience, kindness, goodness, faithfulness, gentleness and self-control.[8] One day, He will take home each one who is trusting in Jesus, to be with Him in heaven. Before that time, if you are a Christian, you have the privilege of serving Him who saved you. A vital first step in this service is baptism.

Baptism

We saw in the preceding chapter that a personal response is required of each of us as we come face to face with Christ. Having responded by believing, trusting in and following Jesus, the next step in your new life is the response of baptism. This is a symbolic sharing in the death, burial and resurrection of Jesus. It is done publicly as a profession of faith in Christ and all that He has done for us. It is the badge of Christian discipleship. If you read the book of Acts you will find many instances of people repenting, believing in Christ and being baptized.[9] Baptism is a vital step in your Christian life, not least because it is done in obedience to Jesus' own command.[10] The Bible tells us that by hearing and obeying the Lord, we build our lives on the Rock and are progressively made more like Christ Himself.[11] Obedience is

God's pathway for the Christian in their desire to 'be holy'; the means is the Holy Spirit, who helps and comforts, who comes alongside us to guide us and help us understand what God has freely given us.[12]

Here are some suggestions that I commend to you as a new believer.

Give God the first day of every week

In the Bible, Sunday, the first day of the week, is set apart as God's day.[13] The Jews kept Saturday as their Sabbath to remind them of the work of the Father in creation. God rested in satisfaction on the seventh day of creation. We keep Sunday as His day, which reminds us not only of the work of the Father in creation, but also of the work of the Son in re-creation (He rose from the dead on the Sunday morning), and the work of the Holy Spirit in procreation (He came upon the gathered Christians seven weeks later, at Pentecost). There are jobs that have to be done every day of the week, including Sunday. Jesus spoke about works of mercy or necessity and, of course, there will be Christians involved in these. However, every Christian needs the company of other Christians so that together they can worship, work and witness for God.

Find a church: (i) that believes the Bible; (ii) that preaches Jesus Christ and Him crucified and risen; (iii) where you can meet with brothers and sisters in Christ; and (iv) where you can take others for whom you are praying. No church is perfect; after all, Christians are simply forgiven sinners. But a church is not really a church if 'another gospel' is preached, which does not focus attention on 'Jesus Christ, the one who was crucified'.[14]

As you go to church with others, you will learn more about God and how to worship Him. Take notes from the sermons. If there is anything you don't understand, ask questions and start to become familiar with the Bible. D.L. Moody, the evangelist, said: 'Carry your Bible to church and you will preach a sermon a mile long!' If you are able, as soon as you can, start to attend a midweek Bible study and prayer meeting and get involved in working for the cause of Christ. There are many churches praying that God will send them godly workers. However, you should not feel that you have to get involved with every church project in order to be accepted by God or the church. Nor need you feel disapproval if you cannot attend all meetings. God Himself is your priority, and you probably have family and friendships to cultivate too.

Sunday afternoon and evening can be a time of reading for spiritual growth. Reading is to the mind what eating is to the body. Reading good Christian biographies feeds the mind, fills the heart and fires the spirit. It is often the antidote to lethargic living and dull conversation. Although not inspired in the same way as the Bible, many Christians have found the right biography to be spiritually uplifting. God has used books as the instrument to call Christians into sacrificial unstinting service. The books I have listed below, I would consider as investments for life. They are the beginner's basic diet and the mature Christian's reminder of the kind of life to which we are called. It may take quite some time to get through them all, but biography has been used of God to keep Christians spiritually sharp.

I therefore recommend these to you. Sell your coat to buy them! Set aside time to read them.

1. Roger Steer, *J. Hudson Taylor: A Man in Christ* (Sevenoaks: OMF, 1993).
2. C.H. Spurgeon (autobiography), Volume One, *The Early Years* and Volume Two, *The Full Harvest* (Carlisle, Pennsylvania: Banner of Truth Trust, 1967, 1973).

3. A.T. Pierson, *George Müller of Bristol* (Peabody, MA: Hendrickson, 2008).

4. J.C. Ryle, *Five English Reformers* (Carlisle, Pennsylvania: Banner of Truth Trust, 1960).

5. John Pollock, *Moody Without Sankey* (Fearn, Tain: Christian Focus, 2010).

6. Andrew Bonar, *Robert Murray McCheyne: Memoirs and Remains* (Carlisle, Pennsylvania: Banner of Truth Trust, 1966).

7. Jonathan Edwards, ed., *The Life and Diary of David Brainerd* (Grand Rapids, MI: Baker Book House, 1989).

8. Elisabeth Elliot, *Through Gates of Splendour* (Carlisle: Authentic Media, 1988).

9. Warren Wiersbe, *50 People Every Christian Should Know* (Ada, MI: Baker Books, 2009).

10ofthose.com sell only Christian books which can be trusted as being true to the Bible and the historic Christian faith.

You will soon find that Christians, despite all their failings, can become the finest friends in the world. Christians are great fun to be with, for, after all, they are at peace with God and enjoy His peace in their hearts. However, don't just fritter away time with them, but talk of spiritual things and seek to serve God together.

The Bible makes mention of the phrase 'one another' many times. It says, for example, that Christians should:

• Love one another
• Bear with one another
• Be kind to one another
• Forgive one another
• Comfort one another
• Consider one another
• Pray for one another

- Show compassion to one another
- Be hospitable to one another.[15]

Often the zeal and joy of a new believer can be a rich blessing and challenge to those who have been Christians for some years – 'not forsaking the assembling of ourselves together ... but exhorting one another,' says the Bible.[16]

Give God the first minutes of every day

Never neglect daily Bible reading and private prayer. Ideally it is best to give God the first few minutes of our day. But, of course, He knows that this is not always possible, due to some people's circumstances. If this is the case, then try to find another part of the day which is more appropriate. However, it is important that you do set aside a specific time. The Bible is the major way that God has revealed to us His character and His will. God's Word is living and powerful, and through it God will speak to you. The more you get to know Him, the more you will love Him and want to spend time with Him. Prayer is equally vital in drawing close to God. Prayer is communion with God: you speaking with Him, and He with you. God will speak to you principally through the Bible, and you can speak to God through prayer. The Bible and prayer are vital for the Christian life. The Bible will keep you from wrongdoing, or wrongdoing will keep you from the Bible.

As well as reading some verses every day, it is good to study the Scriptures systematically. I would recommend reading through the New Testament chapter by chapter first of all. You could then read the Old and New Testaments together, perhaps a portion of each every day. There are helpful Bible-reading notes suitable for all ages and stages in the Christian life. 'Like newborn babies, you must crave pure spiritual milk so that you will grow into a full experience of salvation.'[17]

Underline verses that 'speak' to you and write down thoughts that come to mind as you read. Many people find writing notes in the margin of their Bibles is helpful, whilst others prefer to use a separate notebook. Memorize key Bible verses. David knew the value of this discipline: 'I have hidden your word in my heart, that I might not sin against you.'[18] Also pass on verses to others – after all, expression deepens impression! Unless you become a man or woman of the Bible, you may be thrown around by new trends of doctrine, which quickly come and go.

Archbishop Usher said, 'My greatest delight in life is to be in a nook with the Book!' If you can get into the daily, dogged discipline of Bible reading, you will find it becomes a delight.

When I became a Christian at the age of 15 in the Lebanon, the man who led me to Christ, the Reverend Hagop Sagherian, said, 'Make an appointment to meet with God at a particular time and place, and never keep God waiting!' It was good advice. Hudson Taylor said, 'A person may be dedicated and devoted but if ill-disciplined, he or she will be useless.'

Don't necessarily expect verses and thoughts to jump out at you, but as you pray and read your Bible, God will teach you truths that will leave abiding and life-transforming impressions on you.

All relationships involve two-way communication. Turn the things you have read into prayer. All that you read in the Bible ask God to help you obey.

In prayer, thank God for all He has done and praise Him for who He is. Pray for your family, friends, church and country, as well as your own needs. Having a prayer notebook can be helpful so that each day we have names of people for whom we are going to pray. God hears and delights to answer prayer. Jesus said:

Keep on asking, and you will receive what you ask for. Keep on seeking, and you will find. Keep on knocking, and the door will be opened to you. For everyone who asks, receives. Everyone who seeks, finds. And to everyone who knocks, the door will be opened. You parents – if your children ask for a loaf of bread, do you give them a stone instead? Or if they ask for a fish, do you give them a snake? Of course not! So if you sinful people know how to give good gifts to your children, how much more will your heavenly Father give good gifts to those who ask him.[19]

If you note down your prayer requests, you will soon find that God is answering prayer, not always in the way that you would imagine, but always for your good and His renown.

When you do sin, confess it to God at once, then trust that it is forgiven, as God promised. A child who is naughty, whether deliberately or unintentionally, does not cease to be the child of their father because of their misdemeanour. Likewise, you have not lost your position as a child of God, but until there is confession and forgiveness, you have lost your close fellowship with Him; wrongdoing always causes separation. The Bible says: 'But if we confess our sins to him, he is faithful and just to forgive us our sins and to cleanse us from all wickedness.'[20]

However, this is not an excuse for us to do wrong. The Bible warns that: 'You will always harvest what you plant. Those who live only to satisfy their own sinful nature will harvest decay and death from that sinful nature. But those who live to please the Spirit will harvest everlasting life from the Spirit.'[21]

Bishop J.C. Ryle said, 'Never expect sin, never excite sin and never excuse sin.' Though sin may be forgiven, its consequences and scars may remain.

This daily 'quiet time' or 'meeting with God' will become the highlight of your day as you spend time with Him. There is no substitute for that precious time.

Give God the first portion of all you have

Giving to God involves not just our finances but our possessions, time and talents; in fact, all that we are and have. Jesus, who was rich in heaven, became poor for us.[22] He was born in a borrowed manger, preached from a borrowed boat, rode to Jerusalem on a borrowed donkey, borrowed a coin to make a point about allegiances, and was buried in a borrowed tomb. He said, 'Foxes have dens to live in, and birds have nests, but the Son of Man has no place even to lay his head.'[23]

He set an example of sacrifice for those He loved. Nobody will compel you or check up on your giving as a Christian. However, there is great joy in being able to meet the needs of others through what God has given to us. Jesus said, 'It is more blessed to give than to receive.'[24] We should do this systematically, sacrificially, and cheerfully. What is more, God has promised that when we give to His work and people in this way, He will open 'the windows of heaven for you. [He] will pour out a blessing so great you won't have enough room to take it in!'[25]

There are great needs in the world. It is vital that all hear the good news that Jesus came into the world to save men and women. We should do everything we can to help in the great cause of passing on the gospel, the commission that Jesus gave to all disciples. To give you vision for what God is doing in other parts of the world, you could start to read a missionary magazine and pray for the work of God overseas. Write to me via the publisher if you would like suggestions of such ministries. Remember that wherever you are now, you are surrounded by needy, hurting people. In many countries Christians are suffering for their faith. We can help to support them practically, as well as by praying. And always keep your ear tuned to the Holy Spirit – He may call you to go yourself.

Christians have always sought to follow Christ's example of caring for the sick and underprivileged. So many of the great social reformers, as well as the founders of hospitals, schools and orphanages, have been Christians. As believers we are to love God and our neighbours; this is the royal law or the law 'that sets you free' as the Bible calls it.[26] To be involved in the work to which God directs us is part of our Christian service.[27]

Give God the first consideration in every decision

God will guide you in all the decisions you have to make if you pray, obey His Word and wait for His perfect timing. He will never lead you against what He has already expressly commanded in the Bible.

In your prayers, humbly remind God of these promises in His Word and ask Him to lead you:

I will guide you along the best pathway for your life. I will advise you and watch over you.[28]

Trust in the LORD with all your heart; do not depend on your own understanding. Seek his will in all you do, and he will show you which path to take.[29]

The LORD will guide you continually, giving you water when you are dry and restoring your strength. You will be like a well-watered garden, like an ever-flowing spring.[30]

If you need wisdom, ask our generous God, and he will give it to you. He will not rebuke you for asking. But when you ask him, be sure that your faith is in God alone. Do not waver, for a person with divided loyalty is as unsettled as a wave of the sea that is blown and tossed by the wind.[31]

If ever you are in doubt as to whether something is right or wrong, ask these three questions:

1. Will it hinder the growth of my spiritual life? The Bible says: 'let us strip off every weight that slows us down, especially the sin that so easily trips us up'.[32]
2. Could it influence someone else in the wrong direction? The Bible says: 'But you must be careful so that your freedom does not cause others with a weaker conscience to stumble.'[33]
3. Will it displease God? The Bible says: 'So whether you eat or drink, or whatever you do, do it all for the glory of God.'[34]

Pray about it and God will show you what to do. If you are still in doubt, hold back. We are to aim to be as holy as it is possible to be in this world.

Give God the first place in your heart
The Christian is the dwelling place of God Himself. Whereas He once came among His people in a tabernacle, and later a temple built with hands, now He dwells within each individual believer by His Holy Spirit:

Don't you realize that your body is the temple of the Holy Spirit, who lives in you and was given to you by God? You do not belong to yourself, for God bought you with a high price. So you must honour God with your body.[35]

We read: 'we have all been baptized into one body by one Spirit, and we all share the same Spirit'.[36]

Because we are His and He is ours, we are 'complete' in Him.[37] Every Christian should pray that Jesus 'is first in everything'.[38]

The Holy Spirit living within is like floodlights on a football pitch, taking the attention from them on to someone else. The Holy Spirit makes much of Christ.[39]

Share the gospel with others by the things you say and the way you live. Never be a secret disciple, but make it your constant aim to introduce others to Christ. The Bible says: 'Instead, you must worship Christ as Lord of your life. And if someone asks about your Christian hope, always be ready to explain it. But do this in a gentle and respectful way.'[40]

Jesus said: 'Everyone who acknowledges me publicly here on earth, I will also acknowledge before my Father in heaven' and 'Go into all the world and preach the Good News to everyone.'[41] Jesus will make you a 'fisher of men' if you follow Him.

Don't allow wrongdoing, laziness or diversions to distract you from the centrality of Christ. Keep trusting Jesus, your living Saviour, in every moment of doubt, temptation or difficulty. He is your constant companion. Ask Him and He will take you through every situation. The Bible says:

> *Give all your worries and cares to God, for he cares about you.*[42]

> *Don't be afraid, for I am with you. Don't be discouraged, for I am your God. I will strengthen you and help you. I will hold you up with my victorious right hand.*[43]

You can never out-give Him who has given His all for us. God says, 'I will honour those who honour me'.[44] He will meet your every need, be it of the body, soul or spirit, material, temporal or eternal.

If you are tempted to doubt, remind yourself of God's precious promises to be found throughout the Bible, and how every one is 'yes' in Christ.[45]

In triumph and jubilation Paul wrote:

> *Can anything ever separate us from Christ's love? Does it mean he no longer loves us if we have trouble or calamity, or are*

persecuted, or hungry, or destitute, or in danger, or threatened with death? (As the Scriptures say, 'For your sake we are killed every day; we are being slaughtered like sheep.') No, despite all these things, overwhelming victory is ours through Christ, who loved us. And I am convinced that nothing can ever separate us from God's love. Neither death nor life, neither angels nor demons, neither our fears for today nor our worries about tomorrow – not even the powers of hell can separate us from God's love. No power in the sky above or in the earth below – indeed, nothing in all creation will ever be able to separate us from the love of God that is revealed in Christ Jesus our Lord.[46]

NOTES

1. 2 Corinthians 5:17
2. 1 Peter 1:16
3. 2 Peter 1:3
4. Luke 9:23; 2 Timothy 3:12
5. 'Trust and Obey', John Henry Sammis, 1846–1919
6. 1 Peter 1:8
7. See Romans 8:29
8. Galatians 5:22–23
9. Acts 2:38,41; 8:12–13,36–38; 9:18; 10:47–48; 16:31–34; 18:8
10. Matthew 28:19
11. Matthew 7:24; John 17:17; 1 Peter 1:22
12. 1 Corinthians 2:12
13. Acts 20:7; 1 Corinthians 16:2
14. 1 Corinthians 2:2. Read Galatians 1:8–9
15. John 13:34, Ephesians 4:2, Ephesians 4:32, 1 Thessalonians 4:18, Hebrews 10:24, James 5:16, 1 Peter 3:8 and 1 Peter 4:9, NKJV

16. Hebrews 10:25, NKJV
17. 1 Peter 2:2
18. Psalm 119:11
19. Matthew 7:7–11
20. 1 John 1:9
21. Galatians 6:7–8
22. 2 Corinthians 8:9
23. Luke 9:58
24. Acts 20:35
25. Malachi 3:10
26. James 2:8; 1:25
27. 1 Thessalonians 1:3; 2 Thessalonians 1:11
28. Psalm 32:8
29. Proverbs 3:5–6
30. Isaiah 58:11
31. James 1:5–6
32. Hebrews 12:1
33. 1 Corinthians 8:9
34. 1 Corinthians 10:31
35. 1 Corinthians 6:19–20
36. 1 Corinthians 12:13
37. Colossians 2:10
38. Colossians 1:18
39. John 16:14
40. 1 Peter 3:15–16
41. Matthew 10:32; Mark 16:15
42. 1 Peter 5:7
43. Isaiah 41:10
44. 1 Samuel 2:30
45. 2 Corinthians 1:20
46. Romans 8:35–39

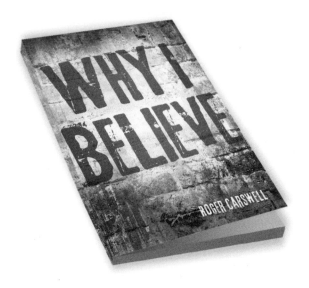

10Publishing is the publishing house of 10ofThose. It is committed to producing quality Christian resources that are biblical and accessible.

www.10ofthose.com is our online retail arm selling thousands of quality books at discounted prices.

For information contact: info@10ofthose.com or check out our website: www.10ofthose.com